ASTRID

# Herbal Remedies

## & Natural Medicine Essentials

Grow & Prepare Infusions, Tinctures, & Oils for Better Health & Wellness

48 Techniques & Tips to Use Plants & Herbs for Holistic Healing

ALL IN 1

# Table of Contents

# Introduction

When you have a headache, the quickest fix you may think for your problem is digesting a pill. *For an upset stomach?* Another pill. *Anxiety?* Yet another. With all these synthetic drugs you often depend upon, while effective, such pills may come with side effects and miss addressing the root causes of your ailments. *But did you know that the best solutions often lie in nature's simplest offerings?*

Centuries ago, an approach promised holistic healing and a deeper connection to the earth—*herbal remedies and natural medicines.* Such a time-honored tradition taps into the curative properties of plants. This book is a gateway to that realm, offering a comprehensive guide to the art and science of herbalism.

As someone with a life dedicated to understanding and advocating holistic health—*one that encompasses the physical, mental, and spiritual dimensions*—all years of discoveries and experiences were poured into this book. Each page contains techniques, tips, and strategies to empower you to take control of your well-being. Learn that wellness through holistic practices is not just about treating symptoms. Instead, it is about understanding your body, mind, spirit, and the world. Beyond that, this book contains information to practice crafting herbal tea concoctions that soothe the body and soul.

Everything to have holistic well-being is within your reach; immerse yourself in the wisdom from this book. Let the ancient secrets of plants and herbs transform your life.

# Chapter 1

# Foundations of Herbal Remedies

From ancient civilizations to modern medicine, using plants and herbs for healing has a long and rich history. The first chapter will illuminate the evolution of herbal practices across cultures and periods. Beginning with the earliest documented uses of medicinal plants, you will uncover how knowledge was preserved and transferred between different groups throughout history.

Beyond that, learn about the spiritual beliefs intertwined with herbalism, including the reverence many cultures had for plants as sacred living entities. Chapter 1 also highlights herbal tribes from various continents, describing their strong bonds with nature. The closing sections then offer useful guidance on when to choose herbal medicine versus Western medicine and how the two can often complement each other.

## Roots of Herbal Practices

Before the inception of hospitals filled with advanced machinery and synthetic drugs, a simpler yet effective natural medicine existed: herbs. Nature, with its bountiful offerings, acted as the primary physician, providing remedies for a multitude of ailments. The origins and propagation of herbal practices are a testament to human ingenuity and a homage to nature's boundless generosity.

## *Earliest Uses*

Egyptians understood the healing power that a plant contains. For instance, garlic was not merely a culinary delight but was also revered for its ability to bolster strength and ward off diseases. Similarly, the Greeks were not far behind in botanical knowledge. Willow bark, for example, is used by Greeks as a go-to remedy as it has salicylic acid. And, of course, the Chinese have these ancient scrolls that are replete with references to various herbs—many of which form the core of Traditional Chinese Medicine that is still practiced and revered today.

## *Transfer of Knowledge*

Like water flowing from one place to another, so does knowledge. *But how did the understanding of herbs traverse continents and epochs?*

Ancient civilizations were not isolated entities. Through wars, explorations, trade, and migrations, they were constantly in a state of flux and interaction. And with these interactions came the exchange of knowledge, including the medicinal uses of plants.

Scribes, scholars, and healers would meticulously document their findings. Over time, these scattered notes morphed into comprehensive manuscripts, scrolls, and books. Such tomes of wisdom did not merely sit on lofty shelves gathering dust but were actively referenced and expanded upon.

*"De Materia Medica"* is an exemplary example of knowledge transfer. Penned by the Greek physician Dioscorides in the 1st century AD, this monumental work did not just remain confined to Greece. Its acclaim spread across continents, becoming the gold standard reference for herbal remedies in Europe for over a millennium and a half.

## Core Spiritual Beliefs

Herbal healing is about how the soul connects with nature and how the spirit moves with the Earth's beat.

### *Plants as Sacred Beings*

The divinity of plants is believed to be universal and timeless as each pulsed with a spirit, essence, and divine energy. Such sentiment remained consistent across diverse landscapes and epochs.

In herbal healing lies a thread that connects the physical to the ethereal: *spirituality*. While the leaves, roots, and flowers played their part in healing the body, their essence was believed to resonate with the human spirit. For countless ancient cultures, dabbling with plants was also a voyage into spiritual rejuvenation and transformation.

Native Americans exemplify this belief with their connection to the land. To them, every leaf and petal was infused with a spirit. Rituals, often elaborate and deeply symbolic, preceded such actions. These ceremonies ensured that the spirit of the plant was honored, appeased, and remained unscathed. Similarly, in the lush terrains of Asia, plants like the sacred basil *(Tulsi)* in India were revered for their medicinal properties, the deities they represented, and the cosmic energies they harbored.

### *Healing as a Holistic Approach*

Herbalists perceived the body, mind, and spirit. And for true healing to manifest, all these facets needed to be in harmony.

When one consumed an herbal brew, it was not just the body that imbibed its benefits. The spirit too, absorbed its essence. For instance, a tea infused with chamomile not only soothes the throat or aids digestion, it also calms the spirit, dispels negativity, and realigns the energies. The philosophy is that healing is not just about curing symptoms but restoring balance and harmony to the entire being.

### *The Importance of Environment in Health*

Human interaction with the environment plays a role in health. Clean air, access to pure water, and a toxin-free living space influence well-being. The emotional environment—*the company you keep and your daily experiences*—impacts your health. Positive, loving relationships and a supportive community can heal like any herb. But loneliness, for example, leads to various health issues. Beyond recommending stress-relieving herbs, a holistic healer might advise joining community groups, adopting a pet, or seeking counseling.

## Prominent Herbal Tribes

Throughout history, many tribes across continents have lived in harmony with nature, drawing sustenance, shelter, and spiritual guidance from the environment. These tribes' bond with nature encompasses a dependency on resources and a deep spiritual, cultural, and emotional connection. Such diverse lifestyles and beliefs exemplify a harmonious coexistence with nature.

### *The Native Americans*

The Native Americans consist of a myriad of tribes, including the Navajo, Cherokee, and Lakota, to name a few. Each tribe shares some common cultural threads and has its distinct identity, language, and traditions.

Historically, Native Americans were hunters, gatherers, and farmers. The tribe's livelihoods were deeply intertwined with the land, following the migratory patterns of buffalo or cultivating the *"Three*

*Sisters" (corn, beans, and squash).* Spiritual ceremonies and rituals, many of which honored the Earth and its bounties, punctuated their lives.

For these tribes, the *"Mother Earth"* concept was integral to their belief systems. This ethos manifested in their sustainable practices, ensuring they took what they needed and gave back to the environment in reciprocity.

## *The Aboriginals of Australia*

In the rugged terrains of Australia, the Aboriginal tribes have thrived for over 65,000 years, making them the world's oldest living civilization. The term *"Aboriginal"* encompasses diverse groups, each with its language, customs, and territories. These groups, spanning the entire continent, are as varied as the Australian landscape.

Traditionally, aboriginals were hunter-gatherers with a life dictated by the seasons, the availability of food, and the spiritual significance of places and events. Dreamtime stories, a unique aspect of their culture, narrate the origins of the Earth and its creatures, setting the moral and social framework for the community.

The Aboriginals see themselves as part of the land. Underpinned by the Dreamtime, their beliefs emphasize the interconnectedness of all living things. Their sustainable hunting and gathering practices reflect this bond with nature, ensuring the land's vitality for future generations.

## *African Tribes*

Africa, a continent of unparalleled diversity, is home to numerous tribes, each enriching the land with its unique culture and wisdom.

Among the many tribes, the Zulu, Maasai, and San stand out for their distinctive cultures and practices. While the Zulu are primarily found in South Africa, the Maasai inhabit parts of Kenya and Tanzania, and the San, often referred to as Bushmen, reside in the Kalahari Desert.

The Zulu are historically cattle herders with a rich warrior tradition. The Maasai, known for their vibrant red attire and beaded jewelry, are semi-nomadic pastoralists. The San, on the other hand, are one of the oldest populations on Earth and are skilled hunter-gatherers.

For African tribes, nature is both a provider and a spiritual entity. The Maasai, for example, believe that God gave them cattle, making the pastoralist lifestyle sacred. The San, with their deep knowledge of the Kalahari, have an innate understanding of plants and animals, using them sustainably for food, medicine, and tools.

## Principles of Holistic Healing

In healing, a philosophy believes in treating the whole person rather than isolated symptoms. This approach, known as holistic healing, views the individual as an integrated whole of the physical, emotional, and spiritual dimensions.

### *Treating the Root, Not Just Symptoms*

When you have a weed in your garden, *do you trim its leaves or pull it out from the root?* Similarly, herbal healing emphasizes addressing the root cause of an ailment rather than just masking the symptoms.

Usually, when one encounters ailments, the immediate inclination is to alleviate the discomfort. However, quick relief often masks the deeper issues lurking beneath. In holistic healing, there is a clarion call to shift focus from the superficial to the foundational.

*Consider an iceberg.* The visible tip above the water's surface might be easily seen, but the colossal mass beneath holds the true essence. Similarly, symptoms are the tangible tip we notice, while the underlying causes remain submerged, often unnoticed. Traditional medicinal practices frequently target the tip, the evident symptoms. However, holistic healing ventures beneath, into the depths, targeting the entirety of the iceberg.

## The Importance of Understanding the Cause

Every symptom is a language, a signal the body communicates, urging attention. However, attending only to the symptom is like muting an alarm without addressing the fire that triggered it.

Taking the analogy of a garden, when plants wither, merely spraying water on the leaves offers temporary respite. But nurturing the roots ensures lasting vitality. In the context of health, recurring headaches, for instance, might be an overt discomfort. The holistic approach might look into causes like stress, diet, or even posture. *Consider chronic fatigue.* While conventional medicine might prescribe energy boosters or caffeine pills, a holistic healer might look at sleep patterns, dietary habits, emotional stressors, or environmental factors.

## Long-term Solutions over Quick Fixes

Addressing root causes offers solutions that are soothing and curative. *Consider an individual battling with persistent headaches.* Conventional treatments might recommend painkillers, providing immediate relief. However, if a holistic practitioner identifies chronic stress as the culprit, the treatment paradigm shifts. Instead of a mere pill, the recommendation might encompass meditation, yoga, or lifestyle modifications. Such interventions alleviate headaches and address the stress, ensuring long-term relief and improved overall well-being.

## *The Holistic Triad*

While powerful individually, the body, mind, and spirit achieve their full potential when in sync with the others, leading to genuine health and well-being.

### The Body

While the physical form is the most tangible and evident aspect of your being, holistic healing recognizes its depth beyond mere structure. The body is not just about muscles, bones, and organs. It is about how these components work in harmony, ensuring vitality and health.

Within our body lies a symphony of circulatory, respiratory, digestive, and other systems. Holistic healing underscores the importance of these systems working in optimal synchronization. For instance, a robust cardiovascular system is not just about a strong heart but also about clean arteries and efficient blood flow, nourishing every cell.

### The Mind

Often termed the control center, our mind dictates how we perceive and respond to the world. It is the hub of thoughts, emotions, memories, and beliefs. In the realm of holistic healing, the health of the mind is as pivotal as the health of the body.

Consider this: A persistent belief in unworthiness can lead to stress, which in turn can manifest as high blood pressure or digestive issues. Such is the power of the mind. Holistic healing thus emphasizes therapies like meditation, counseling, or even journaling to ensure mental clarity and emotional balance.

### The Spirit

While the body and mind are bound by the tangible realm, the spirit soars in the ethereal. It is the beacon that connects us to the cosmos, a higher power, or the profound energies of the universe.

Often underestimated, the spiritual aspect plays a crucial role in holistic healing. For instance, practices like prayer, meditation, or even simple acts of gratitude can have therapeutic effects. By nurturing our spiritual side through religious practices, nature walks, or artistic endeavors, we pave the way for deep-rooted healing and inner tranquility.

## *The Role of Environment in Health*

Delving into holistic healing reveals that health is not solely the product of your internal state. While the harmony between body, mind, and spirit sets the stage, the surrounding environment profoundly influences the play. In this section, you explore the integral role of the external world in influencing and molding your overall health and well-being.

### Physical Surroundings

Homes, workplaces, and even recreational spaces echo the state of health. A cluttered room, for instance, might mirror a cluttered mind, leading to feelings of overwhelm and stress. On the other hand, a clean, organized space can instill a sense of calm and order.

Beyond your immediate surroundings, the quality of the air you breathe and the food you eat is also important. Polluted air introduces toxins, while fresh, clean air rejuvenates your body. Similarly, processed foods can introduce harmful elements into your system, whereas organic, whole foods nourish your body, setting the foundation for optimal health.

### Emotional Environment

Human beings are inherently social creatures. The relationships we cultivate, whether familial, friendly, or professional, can serve as a lifeline or a burden. Toxic, draining relationships can manifest in the form of emotional and even physical ailments. In contrast, positive, nurturing relationships can be the balm that heals wounds, both seen and unseen.

The emotions and energies exchanged in relationships ripple effect on our health. Constant exposure to negativity can dampen our spirit, leading to ailments like depression or anxiety. In contrast, supportive and loving relationships bolster our emotional resilience, often translating into improved physical health.

### Connecting with Nature

Amidst the hustle and bustle of modern life, nature stands as a silent healer. The rustling leaves, the rhythmic waves, and the gentle breeze all have a therapeutic essence. Holistic healing recognizes this and emphasizes the importance of regular communion with nature.

Spending time in natural settings, be it dense forests, serene lakes, or expansive beaches, can work wonders. Nature has an uncanny ability to reduce stress, enhance mental clarity, and rejuvenate the spirit. It is not just about the scenic beauty but the energy and vibrations that nature emanates.

## Western vs. Herbal Medicine

In health and healing, two dominant perspectives emerge: Western medicine, which is often associated with modern scientific practices, and herbal medicine, which is deeply rooted in ancient traditions and the power of nature. While both have merits, understanding their core philosophies and applications can empower individuals to make informed health decisions. This section looks into the foundational tenets, shedding light on their differences and guiding you on when to choose which approach.

## *The Mechanistic Approach of Western Medicine*

Navigating the complexities of health and wellness, Western medicine is a pillar of modern healthcare, adopting a mechanistic view of the human body. *What exactly does this mean, and how does it influence the approach to healing?*

### Unraveling the Body's Mechanisms

Central to the Western medical model is the perspective that the human body functions like a complex, intricate machine. Each organ, tissue, and cell has a specific role, working in harmony to maintain optimal health. When something goes awry, the mechanistic approach dictates a thorough investigation to pinpoint the faulty component, akin to a mechanic diagnosing a malfunction in a car.

This detailed analysis extends to understanding diseases and disorders at a microscopic level. The goal is to uncover the underlying biological or chemical imbalance, providing a clear target for intervention. This method has led to remarkable breakthroughs in disease management and treatment options, saving countless lives and improving the quality of life for many.

### Advancements and Specializations

The mechanical model has paved the way for incredible medical technology and knowledge advancements. Today, we possess the tools to delve deep into the body's workings, identifying issues with precision and speed that were once thought impossible.

This approach has also led to an unprecedented level of specialization in medicine. Some doctors focus solely on the heart, others on the brain, and some dedicate their entire careers to studying a single type of cancer. This specialization ensures that patients receive care from individuals with an extensive understanding of their ailment, fostering better treatment outcomes.

However, it is worth noting that while this specialization has its advantages, it can sometimes lead to a siloed approach to health, where the focus is so narrow that the broader picture of the patient's overall well-being might be overlooked.

## Pharmacological Solutions

In Western medicine, pharmaceuticals reign supreme. These drugs, born from rigorous research and clinical trials, are designed to target specific biological pathways to rectify imbalances, kill invading pathogens, or mitigate symptoms. This approach has led to life-saving treatments and is a testament to the power of modern science.

From antibiotics that combat bacterial infections to anti-inflammatory drugs that ease pain and swelling, pharmaceuticals have become integral to contemporary healthcare. Their precision and potency make them powerful allies in the fight against disease.

Yet, acknowledge that this reliance on drugs also comes with potential downsides. The possibility of side effects, interactions with other medications, and the issue of antibiotic resistance are all facets that require careful consideration. Moreover, the focus on treating symptoms rather than addressing the root cause of an ailment is a point of contention and an aspect where Western medicine can potentially learn from its herbal counterpart.

### *The Wholistic Perspective of Herbalism*

In a world dominated by quick fixes and compartmentalized solutions, herbalism offers a holistic approach to health. Unlike other forms, it does not view ailments in isolation or the body as a mere collection of parts. Instead, herbalism sees each individual as a symphony of interconnected physical, emotional, and spiritual aspects. With its holistic philosophy, herbalism invites you to see health and healing in a new light. It encourages a return to nature, urging you to trust its wisdom and embrace its offerings.

## Harnessing Nature's Pharmacy

At the heart of herbalism is an unwavering faith in the healing properties of plants. It is the belief that within nature lies a vast pharmacy ready to cater to our diverse health needs. Every plant element can offer therapeutic benefits, from the roots buried deep within the earth to the leaves that dance in the wind. As previously mentioned, turmeric is a testament to this, offering potent anti-inflammatory effects.

## Addressing the Root Cause

The beauty of herbal medicine is its aim to treat the core of the problem and not just its manifestations. In the modern medical landscape, treatments are often tailored to suppress symptoms. However, herbalism seeks to uncover and address the underlying imbalances. To elucidate, instead of merely providing relief from a recurrent headache, an herbalist might recommend herbs that target its root causes, such as stress or hormonal imbalances.

## The Mind-Body Connection

In herbal practices, there is a deep understanding that physical health is closely tied to mental and emotional well-being. This means that our thoughts and feelings greatly affect our overall health. Herbalism goes beyond just recommending plants for physical issues. It often merges with other methods like meditation or counseling for a comprehensive approach to healing. This emphasizes the belief that true healing comes from balancing the mind, body, and spirit.

## *When to Choose Which Approach*

In the world of health and wellness, many find themselves at a junction, deciding between the route of Western medicine or venturing into the holistic world of herbalism. This section guides you through this complex choice.

### Acute vs. Chronic Conditions

The nature and urgency of a health condition often dictate the best approach. Western medicine is unparalleled in acute ailments—sudden injuries, infections, or severe medical conditions. Its rapid response and advanced technologies can mean the difference between life and death.

Conversely, when we discuss chronic conditions, the picture shifts. These ailments persist over time, often rooted in lifestyle, environmental factors, or systemic imbalances. Here, herbalism, focusing on restoring balance and nurturing the body, can provide lasting relief. Conditions like digestive disorders, stress-induced ailments, or hormonal imbalances might benefit from the herbal touch.

### Complementary Paths

The realm of health is not strictly black and white. There is a vast gray area where Western medicine and herbalism coexist harmoniously. This integrative approach can offer the best of both worlds.

Consider someone grappling with diabetes. While they might rely on insulin and other medications for blood sugar management, they could also incorporate herbs like cinnamon or fenugreek, known for their blood sugar-regulating properties. It is about creating a therapeutic synergy, where each approach amplifies the other's benefits.

## Informed Choices

The decision to tread the path of Western medicine, herbalism, or a blend of both is deeply personal. Factors like individual beliefs, past experiences, the nature of the ailment, and even cultural influences play a role.

However, central to this decision-making process is being informed. Engaging in research, seeking diverse opinions, and maintaining an open dialogue with healthcare professionals can provide clarity. With the right knowledge, one can confidently choose the best approach to one's unique health needs and personal philosophy.

# CHAPTER 2

# The Global Tapestry of Herbalism

As you embark on this journey through the serene monastery gardens of medieval Europe to the rugged Australian outback, discover how diverse cultures have embraced the gifts of nature. From ancient China and India's time-honored systems to Aboriginal Australians' deep bond with the land, you will uncover the origins, key plants, and traditional practices that have shaped herbal knowledge through the ages. Discover how traditional wisdom is merged with modern science and sustainability to ensure these practices endure. The multitude of cultures covered is a sample of the diverse threads forming the global tapestry of herbalism.

## Chinese and Ayurvedic Herbal Traditions

Throughout the tapestry of human history, various cultures have harnessed the power of nature to heal, rejuvenate, and enhance the human experience. Among these, Chinese and Ayurvedic herbal traditions stand out as two of the most ancient and influential systems. Dive right into these rich traditions to uncover their origins, principles, and the herbal remedies they offer.

## *The Foundations of Traditional Chinese Medicine*

Traditional Chinese medicine is a beacon of ancient medical wisdom, practiced for millennia. It paints a comprehensive picture of health by interweaving the body, environment, and spirit.

As you trace the origins of these traditional Chinese medicines, you will find it deeply anchored in the ancient Chinese philosophy of Daoism. Daoism, with its reverence for the natural world, provides a fitting backdrop. At the core of this philosophy lies the principle of yin and yang. These opposing yet complementary forces represent the innate dualities in nature: the chill of winter versus the warmth of summer or the stillness of night contrasting the activity of day. Just as nature thrives in harmony, their traditional medicines highlight that health flourishes when the body's internal yin and yang are in equilibrium.

Moving from this philosophical foundation, the question arises: *how does traditional Chinese medicine diagnose and address imbalances?*

### Diagnostic Tools

Traditional Chinese medicine employs a set of unique diagnostic tools to ascertain the delicate balance of yin and yang in an individual. The pulse, for instance, is not just a measure of heart rate. To a trained practitioner, it provides nuanced information about various organ systems. The appearance and texture of the tongue, alongside the specific symptoms a person presents, further refine this diagnostic picture. The practitioner gains a window into the body's harmonies and dissonances by understanding these signals.

Having gleaned these insights, the next logical step is to correct these imbalances. And here, nature lends a hand in the form of herbs.

### Herbal Treatment

Just as every individual is unique, so are the herbal treatments prescribed in TCM. Tailored to address specific imbalances, these remedies tap into nature's pharmacy. If one feels constantly drained, they might be introduced to the rejuvenating powers of ginseng. Conversely, those seeking clarity in vision or an immune boost could find allies in goji berries. These are but glimpses of the vast herbal landscape that traditional Chinese medicine navigates. Whether consumed individually or combined into potent formulas, these herbs aim to restore the body's natural equilibrium.

## *Ayurveda and the Doshas*

Navigating through the vast expanse of natural healing traditions, Ayurveda stands out, much like a seasoned sage with tales woven from the fabric of ancient India. Often described as the 'science of life,' Ayurveda is a testament to India's ancient wisdom on health and well-being. At the same time, it shares the holistic vision of traditional Chinese medicine. Ayurveda charts its unique path, deeply rooted in the principles of the five elements and the trinity of doshas.

### Understanding the Doshas

The heartbeat of Ayurveda lies in understanding the interplay of the doshas Vata, Pitta, and Kapha. Imagine these doshas as distinct blueprints, each sketching a combination of the universe's five fundamental elements: ether, air, fire, water, and earth. These blueprints, etched into our being at birth, mold our physique, character, and even our vulnerabilities to specific health concerns.

To bring this concept to life:

- **Vata (Air and Ether):** Picture the wind, swift and unpredictable. Vata individuals often mirror these qualities—they might have a light physique brimming with energy and spontaneity. But when the wind turns stormy, imbalances strike, leading to issues like anxiety or digestive disturbances.

- **Pitta (Fire and Water):** Visualize the midday sun, intense and illuminating. Those with a Pitta constitution often radiate a fiery intellect and have a moderate build. However, when this inner fire rages uncontrolled, it can manifest as inflammation or bursts of anger.
- **Kapha (Water and Earth):** Think of a serene lake or a sturdy mountain. Kapha individuals often exude a sense of calm and stability with a robust physique. But when the waters stagnate or the mountain becomes inert, imbalances like lethargy or excessive weight can set in.

## Herbal Approaches

Ayurveda, in its infinite wisdom, turns to Mother Nature's herbal troves to harmonize the doshas. Each herb has a unique energetic signature that amplifies or pacifies specific dosha qualities. For example, the golden-hued turmeric, with its innate warmth, can melt away excess Kapha. In contrast, like a cool breeze, the refreshing mint can temper an overzealous Pitta.

### *Examples of Herbs*

The annals of TCM and Ayurveda brim with herbal formulations that have offered solace and healing to countless souls. Despite their ancient origins, these remedies find resonance even in today's modern world, serving as a testament to their enduring efficacy.

**Chinese Herbs:**

- **Reishi Mushroom:** Touted as the *"mushroom of immortality,"* Reishi has been revered in TCM for its potential to enhance longevity and improve overall well-being.

- **Schisandra:** This berry, often called the *"five-flavor fruit,"* is believed to possess adaptogenic qualities, helping the body resist stressors and achieve a harmonious state.

**Ayurvedic Herbs:**

- **Brahmi (Bacopa monnieri):** Known as a brain tonic, Brahmi is often employed to sharpen the intellect, enhance memory, and calm the mind.
- **Shatavari:** Often regarded as a female tonic, Shatavari is believed to support reproductive health, nourish the body, and promote vitality.

### Commonalities and the Essence of Healing

Traversing the corridors of TCM and Ayurveda, one discerns an echoing sentiment: the desire to harmonize the individual with the rhythms of nature. Whether it is Schisandra's adaptogenic properties or Shatavari's rejuvenating attributes, the primary objective remains consistent: to usher in balance, invigorate the spirit, and fortify against ailments.

## African Practices and Beliefs

vast African continent, with its rich biodiversity and millennia-old cultures, offers a treasure trove of herbal remedies and medicinal practices. As part of the global tapestry of herbalism, African traditions provide a vibrant thread rich in history, culture, and healing knowledge. In this exploration, you will explore key medicinal plants, delve into sacred rituals, and observe how modernity interfaces with age-old practices.

### *Key Plants*

Every African region boasts a unique flora adapted to its specific climate and terrain. These plants, nurtured under the African sun, have been the pillars of health and well-being for countless generations.

- **Moringa (Moringa oleifera):** Often dubbed the *"Miracle Tree,"* every part of the Moringa plant has medicinal properties. Its leaves are packed with essential nutrients, making it a powerful tonic for general health.
- **Rooibos (Aspalathus linearis):** Exclusive to South Africa's Cederberg region, this red bush makes a caffeine-free tea known for its antioxidant properties and ability to soothe digestive troubles.
- **Baobab (Adansonia):** Revered as the *"Tree of Life,"* the baobab fruit is a powerhouse of Vitamin C. Its pulp can be consumed to boost immunity and enhance energy.

### *Rituals*

The African landscape is a canvas painted with myriad rituals that meld the tangible and the ethereal. In this vast continent, plants are not merely silent spectators; they are potent tools pivotal in rituals that bridge the gap between our world and the unseen dimensions. This section delves into two distinct ritualistic practices that beautifully illustrate this communion.

#### The Iboga Ceremony

Deep within the heart of Gabon, the Bwiti religion reveres a plant whose roots plunge not just into the earth but into the very psyche of its people: *the Iboga.* This plant is not approached casually. When ingested, its bark can unlock gateways to profound spiritual realms.

Imagine a ceremonial setting, illuminated by the soft glow of torches, the air thick with anticipation. As the participants consume the Iboga root bark, guided by seasoned shamans, the ordinary reality starts to blur. Vivid visions unfold, often revealing ancestral spirits or clarifying life's puzzles. For many, this journey, though intense, is akin to several years of therapy compressed into a single night. The ritual, interspersed with songs and stories, ensures that participants are safely guided through their introspective odyssey, emerging with newfound insights.

### Healing Dances

Across the African expanse, from the Sahara's edges to the verdant heart of Congo, dance and music are not mere art forms but medicinal. Envision a village clearing bathed in moonlight, the ground thudding under the weight of rhythmic feet, and the air vibrating with drumbeats.

As the tempo escalates, dancers adorned with beads and symbolic paints lose themselves in the rhythm. Their movements, sometimes frantic, sometimes graceful, channel the energy of the gathering. It is believed that spirits descend at the peak of these dances, using the dancers as vessels. These spirits, benevolent in nature, might offer guidance, bestow blessings, or even heal ailments. Witnesses often describe this spectacle as transcendental, where the boundary between the human and the divine momentarily dissolves.

## *Merging Ancient Wisdom with Contemporary Needs*

As we have journeyed through the ritualistic practices rooted in Africa's rich soils, it becomes evident how intertwined the tangible and ethereal are. Moving forward, this section discusses how such time-honored traditions are finding their space and voice in today's globalized world, ensuring their legacy persists in a rapidly changing landscape.

### Scientific Validation

The global scientific community has focused on the potential within Africa's diverse flora. Plants like Aloe vera, traditionally used for its healing properties on the skin, and the African Potato, believed to bolster the immune system, are now subjects of rigorous scientific study. Through such research, the medicinal benefits of these plants are being endorsed and refined, making them more accessible and acceptable to a global audience. The validation also promises to introduce more of Africa's herbal bounty to the world, strengthening its position in global health and wellness markets.

### Cultural Preservation

However, the winds of modernity bring challenges as well. With younger generations gravitating towards urban centers, there is a risk that the oral traditions of African herbalism may fade. Recognizing this threat, efforts are being made across the continent to document, safeguard, and pass on this invaluable knowledge. Museums, educational institutions, and community initiatives focus on collating and codifying these practices. By marrying modern tools like digital archiving with traditional storytelling sessions, these initiatives aim to ensure that the wealth of African herbalism is not lost to time.

## European Remedies

As the sun cast its golden hue on Europe's cobblestone streets and towering castles during the Middle Ages, another quiet revolution flourished in herb gardens and apothecaries. This era, often darkened by plagues and wars, saw herbs as glimmers of hope, healing wounds, and physical and metaphysical ailments. In this backdrop, monastery gardens thrived as centers of botanical knowledge, while alchemy intertwined mysticism with medicine, and folk traditions passed down herbal wisdom from generation to generation.

### *Monastic Gardens*

In the heart of the medieval era, serene pockets of green emerged within the quiet walls of monasteries. These places were not just realms of spiritual pursuits; they also became the cradles of herbal knowledge and practices.

Monasteries, usually located far from the distractions of urban life, provided the ideal setting for monks to nurture their spiritual lives and the world of plants. Tending to the gardens became a form of meditative practice, aligning with their monastic vows and promoting a lifestyle of simplicity, humility, and connection to the Earth.

These diverse herbariums, resonating with the richness of a botanical library, held an impressive array of herbs. A stroll through one such garden would have been a sensory delight. The soft, silvery leaves of sage would rustle in the breeze, releasing their aromatic oils, while gentle chamomile flowers swayed, their apple-like scent hinting at their calming properties. Each plant, whether the tall-standing fennel or the humble yarrow, had its role in the holistic well-being of the monastic community.

However, the monastic contribution to herbalism did not end with cultivation. Within the silent corridors and candlelit rooms of the monasteries, monks took on the role of scholars. Their sacred texts and herbal manuals are a testament to their dedication. With patient hands, they penned down detailed descriptions of each herb, their uses, and preparation methods. Accompanying these texts were often intricate illustrations, capturing the essence of each plant in vivid detail. These manuscripts, many of which survive today, serve as windows into medieval herbology, showcasing the depth and breadth of knowledge preserved by these monastic communities.

### *Alchemy and Herbology*

Beyond the mystical quest to turn base metals into gold, medieval alchemists delved deep into the mysteries of nature. Their labs, often filled with alembics and retorts, bore witness to early experiments with plants and minerals.

As alchemists sought the Philosopher's Stone, an elusive substance, they distilled plants, believing in their potential to create potent healing elixirs. This led to the extraction of essential oils from herbs, an art still practiced today. Their rigorous methodologies and a sense of wonder laid the groundwork for today's drug discovery processes.

### *Folk Traditions*

European herbal practices find their most vibrant expressions among the people. Folklore weaves tales of herbs, rituals, and nature's enchantments in the continent's charming hamlets and dense woodlands. These practices, born from a harmonious relationship with nature, were not just about curative measures but also preventive care, balance, and connection.

#### Seasonal Celebrations

Each changing season painted Europe's landscape with unique colors and brought forth various plants. These seasonal shifts were not just meteorological phenomena but communal celebration and gratitude moments.

- **Midsummer Magic:** Take, for example, the longest day of the year. Midsummer, with its abundant sunlight, was not merely a day but an event. Communities across Europe believed certain plants, like St. John's wort, imbibed the sun's radiant energy more potently today. Similarly, el-

derflowers, often made into syrups or cordials, were gathered in some regions during this period, believed to boost immunity and ward off colds.
- **Harvest Blessings:** Come autumn, as golden hues draped the fields, celebrations like Lammas or Lughnasadh acknowledged the grain's bounty. At this time, herbs like rosemary were intertwined in wreaths or burnt, their fragrant smoke purifying homes and heralding a prosperous harvest.

## The Sanctuaries of Nature

Throughout Europe, certain spots pulsated with a spiritual energy. They were not always grand cathedrals; sometimes, it was a whispering grove or a serene spring, such as those listed below.

- **Celtic Groves:** In ancient Celtic traditions, groves, especially those of oak trees, were revered. Rituals were held beneath their leafy canopy, with mistletoe, a sacred herb, harvested using a golden sickle for its believed protective and fertility-enhancing powers.
- **Blessed Waters:** Springs and wells, bubbling with clear, cool water, were another focus. People often left offerings or tied cloth strips, symbolizing prayers or wishes. Nearby, watercress or meadowsweet might be harvested, both known for their soothing properties.

## Herbal Charms and Amulets

In the tapestry of Europe's folk traditions, there was a profound recognition of the intangible — the world of energies, spirits, and auras. In this unseen realm, herbs were more than just plants; they served as quiet protectors and guides.

Take mugwort, for example. While its protective qualities are well noted, its magic runs deeper. Across various European regions, people would tuck mugwort under their pillows, hoping it would usher in prophetic dreams. Others would burn it as incense during rituals, seeking insights into the future.

Then, the rowan tree is easily recognized by its striking red berries. When bound with a red thread, its twigs became more than just a part of the tree. They transformed into charms, believed to shield households from ill intentions and negative energies.

## Phytotherapy

Folk traditions of Europe, with their myriad practices, are not relics of the past. They breathe, evolve, and flow, influencing more structured herbal practices. As Europe marched into modernity, the ancient knowledge of plants began to be viewed through a more systematic and scientific lens. Enter phytotherapy, where tradition meets rigorous study.

Unlike the broader umbrella of herbalism, phytotherapy is more specific. It emphasizes the study and application of medicinal plants based on scientific research and clinical trials. While the knowledge of plants like chamomile, thyme, and valerian has been passed down for generations, phytotherapy validates their uses with research, ensuring efficacy and safety. Today, many European countries have integrated phytotherapy into their healthcare systems, with professionals prescribing plant-based remedies alongside or as alternatives to conventional medicines.

One of phytotherapy's advantages is the standardization of herbal preparations, ensuring consistent potency. Moreover, with growing environmental awareness, there is a keen focus on sustainable cultivation and harvesting of medicinal plants.

## Oceanic Herbalism

The oceans and islands of our world are more than just expanses of water and patches of land; they are treasure troves of ancient knowledge and herbal wonders. Delve into the vast realm of Oceanic herbalism, where every island whisper tales of traditional remedies, and the waves carry secrets of the deep. From the navigating prowess of the Polynesians to the timeless bond of the Aboriginals with their land, discover how these ancient cultures harnessed the bounty of nature and the sea. As you voyage through these waters, you will also touch upon the pressing need to safeguard these green treasures for future generations.

### *Polynesians*

The vast expanse of the Pacific Ocean cradles many islands, each bearing unique ecosystems. The Polynesians, masters of navigation, not only charted these waters but also mapped out a rich tapestry of herbal remedies. Here is a glimpse into their rich herbal culture.

- **Nature's Bounty on Islands:** With limited resources, Polynesians learned to utilize every available plant. The noni fruit, for instance, has been a staple in traditional medicine, known for its potential anti-inflammatory and immune-boosting properties.
- **Healers and Traditions:** Every island had its healers or *"kahuna,"* custodians of the herbal lore. Their knowledge was handed down orally, intertwining with myths, legends, and chants, making medicine and culture inseparable.
- **Sea and Plant Synergy:** Living amidst the vast ocean, Polynesian remedies often combine terrestrial and marine ingredients. Rich in minerals and nutrients, the seaweed would be used alongside island plants for various treatments.

### *Aboriginal People*

Australia, an ancient land with unique flora and fauna, is home to the Aboriginal people. Their bond with the land goes back tens of thousands of years, with it, an intricate understanding of the region's medicinal plants. Here, you will see how herbs can be seen in their culture.

- **Dreamtime Stories and Plants:** Aboriginal lore is rich with *"Dreamtime"* stories that explain the origins and uses of various plants. For example, the tea tree, now globally recognized for its antiseptic properties, has been a part of Aboriginal medicine for millennia, its uses narrated through legends.
- **Bush Medicine:** Venturing into the Australian bush reveals a plethora of remedies. The Kakadu plum, for instance, is known for its remarkable vitamin C content, and eucalyptus leaves have been traditionally used for respiratory issues.
- **Nature's Pharmacy:** From the desert to the coast, Aboriginal remedies span various terrains. Whether it is the soothing qualities of aloe vera from arid regions or the anti-fungal properties of certain coastal plants, Aboriginal medicine is a testament to nature's vastness.

### *Sustainability*

While brimming with herbal riches, the oceanic regions are also sensitive ecosystems. With modern-day challenges, the importance of sustainable practices in harvesting and utilizing these resources cannot be overstated.

- **Overharvesting and Its Perils:** Many valuable herbs and marine plants are at risk due to overharvesting. Sustainable practices ensure that these plants can thrive and benefit future generations.

- **Cultural Respect and Rights:** Indigenous communities, be it Polynesians or Aboriginals, hold the keys to many herbal secrets. Recognizing their rights and knowledge and ensuring they benefit from the commercial use of their traditional remedies is a vital aspect of sustainability.
- **Conservation Initiatives:** From establishing marine conservation areas to promoting sustainable farming of medicinal plants, numerous initiatives are underway to protect the oceanic region's herbal heritage.

# Chapter 3

# Getting Started with Herbalism

The world of herbal remedies offers a treasure trove of natural healing, but knowing where to start can be daunting for a beginner. This comprehensive guide is the perfect starting point for anyone new to using herbs for health and wellness. It covers the fundamentals in a clear, accessible way, walking you through selecting herbs, essential preparations and dosages, safety precautions, and more. With the knowledge gained from this introductory guide, you will gain the confidence to start creating your herbal collection and safely incorporate the healing power of herbs into your life.

## Herbal Selection and Preservation

The world of herbal remedies and natural medicine can seem overwhelming to newcomers. Yet, with a few essential guidelines, anyone can confidently embark on this journey. This section discusses the core concepts of selecting and preserving herbs. Even if you have zero knowledge about this topic, you will have a foundational understanding of how to choose the right herbs and keep them potent for longer.

## *Key Herbs and Their Properties*

The vast array of herbs available offers a plethora of healing properties. However, some essential herbs are particularly notable for their effectiveness and versatility.

- **Chamomile:** Renowned for its calming effects, chamomile can be consumed as a tea to aid sleep or soothe digestive problems. Many also find relief from skin irritations using chamomile-infused creams.
- **Echinacea:** Often turned to for immune support, echinacea is a favorite during flu season. Apart from combating colds and respiratory infections, it can promote wound healing when used topically.
- **Turmeric:** This golden herb is more than just a spice. Turmeric's anti-inflammatory properties, largely due to its active component, curcumin, can aid joint health digestion and even offer cardiovascular benefits.
- **Lavender:** Lavender is not only aromatic but also multi-functional. Its calming effects can alleviate stress, anxiety, and insomnia. Antibacterial properties also make it useful in treating minor burns and cuts.
- **Ginger:** Beyond being a spicy treat, ginger can be a savior for your stomach. It is a go-to remedy for nausea, especially during pregnancy or after surgery. Moreover, ginger can combat inflammation and provide pain relief.
- **Peppermint:** A fragrant herb that is much more than just a flavoring for your holiday treats. Consumed as tea or inhaled as an oil, peppermint can relieve headaches, enhance energy, and soothe digestive woes.
- **St. John's Wort:** Primarily known for its mood-boosting qualities, St. John's Wort is often used as a natural remedy for depression, anxiety, and sleep disorders.
- **Ginkgo Biloba:** An ancient herb that is known to improve cognitive functions. It is often consumed to boost mem-

ory and concentration and even to manage symptoms of Alzheimer's in some cases.

- **Milk Thistle:** This herb is a favorite among those concerned about liver health. It can protect against liver diseases and detoxify harmful substances from the body.
- **Aloe Vera:** Often associated with skincare, aloe vera offers benefits beyond treating sunburn. Consumed in juice, it can aid digestion, while its topical application can treat various skin conditions.

## *Sourcing Quality Herbs*

Navigating the vast world of herbal remedies means knowing the properties of various herbs and where and how to source them. The quality and potency of your chosen herbs are pivotal in their effectiveness. Your commitment to quality sourcing enhances the effectiveness of your remedies and contributes to the sustainability of the world's precious ecosystem. Listed below are the factors you should consider when sourcing your herbs.

### Going Organic

Organic herbs are grown without synthetic pesticides, herbicides, or fertilizers. This is beneficial for your health and ensures that the herbs maintain their natural potency and essential medicinal properties.

### How to Spot Organic Herbs?

Always look for certification labels when buying. Certifying bodies like the USDA *(United States Department of Agriculture)* or similar organizations in other countries often provide organic certifications to producers. These labels offer assurance that the herbs meet the required organic standards. Remember, some local growers might follow organic practices even if not certified, so always ask if you are unsure.

## Local Sources

Local herbs are often fresher since they have not traveled long distances. Fresh herbs retain more natural oils, flavors, and medicinal properties. Additionally, buying locally reduces carbon footprint, ensuring the herbs are good for you and the planet.

## Where to Find Local Herbs?

Farmers' markets are a treasure trove of locally grown produce. Not only can you get fresh herbs, but you also have the opportunity to interact directly with the growers. This direct conversation lets you learn about their farming practices, ensuring you get the best quality.

## Ethical and Sustainable

Some herbs risk being overharvested, leading to their potential extinction in the wild. Ethical sourcing ensures that herbs are harvested in a way that allows the plant population to thrive. This is crucial for the environment and ensuring the continued availability of the herbs for future generations.

## What to Look For?

Suppliers who follow ethical and sustainable practices often provide information about their harvesting methods. They might be affiliated with conservation organizations or follow guidelines set by bodies like the United Plant Savers. Do some research, read labels, and do not hesitate to ask suppliers directly about their sourcing practices.

## *Storage*

Just as a gourmet chef is careful about storing ingredients to maintain their flavor, anyone delving into herbalism should be diligent about storing herbs to preserve their medicinal potency. Storing herbs properly can be the difference between a powerful remedy and an ineffective one. Uncover the intricacies of herb storage and how best to ensure longevity and potency below:

### Choose Dark and Dry Storage Areas

Herbs contain various compounds responsible for their medicinal properties. Light, especially direct sunlight, can degrade these compounds, reducing the herb's efficacy. This is why herbs often lose color when exposed to light—a sign of degradation.

On the other hand, moisture is a breeding ground for mold and bacteria. Even a little bit of dampness can spoil your entire stash. Moisture can also lead to the herbs losing their strength as active compounds dissolve.

### Ideal Storage Solutions

Dark glass jars, like amber or cobalt blue, are excellent choices. They shield the herbs from harmful light rays, allowing you to see the contents. Ensure the jars are kept in cupboards or drawers away from heat sources, like stoves or ovens, as heat can also degrade the herbs.

### Use Airtight Containers

Air, especially if humid, can introduce moisture to your herbs. Oxygen in the air can also oxidize and degrade some of the beneficial compounds in herbs. When opting for glass jars, ensure they have a tight-sealing lid. Mason jars or similar jars with rubber gaskets and clasp closures are especially good. Before sealing, ensure the rim of the jar is clean and dry.

### Label and Date

While some herbs are easily recognizable, others, especially when powdered, can look strikingly similar. Without proper labeling, you might use the wrong herb, leading to unintended effects.

### The Importance of Dating

Over time, even well-stored herbs can lose their potency. By dating your stored herbs, you ensure you use them at their peak efficacy. As a general rule, dried herbs maintain their potency for about a year, but this can vary based on the herb and storage conditions.

### How to Label Efficiently

Use clear, legible writing, and if possible, use waterproof labels or markers. Including both the common name and the Latin name of the herb can be helpful, especially if you are dealing with multiple varieties of herbs.

## Herbal Preparations

Just like memories, the potency and freshness of herbs can be preserved, ensuring you harness their maximum benefits long after their usual shelf life. Preservation is not just about increasing longevity; it is about capturing the essence and strength of the herb at its peak. Here is a detailed look into various preservation techniques alongside some popular herbs best suited for each method.

### *Drying*

Drying involves removing all moisture from herbs, preventing mold and bacteria growth.

#### Best Techniques

- **Air Drying:** Herbs are bundled and hung upside down in a dry, well-ventilated area. This method is ideal for herbs with lower moisture content, like rosemary or thyme.
- **Oven Drying:** For those with higher moisture content, like basil, you can lay the herbs on a baking sheet and dry them in an oven to the lowest temperature.
- **Dehydrator:** A more controlled method ideal for herbs like mint or oregano, which might lose color or potency in an oven.

Once dried, store in dark, airtight containers and label with the name and date.

### *Tinctures*

Tincturing is an ancient method used to extract and preserve the medicinal properties of herbs. By immersing herbs in a solvent, typically alcohol or vinegar, the active compounds of the plant are pulled out, resulting in a potent liquid that can be consumed in small doses. Over the years, certain herbs have become favorites in tincturing due to their well-recognized benefits and ease of extraction.

#### Popular Herbs for Tincturing:

Some of these popular herbs and their primary uses are in tincture form.

- **Echinacea:** Echinacea is a top choice for many herbalists to boost the immune system. It is often turned to during flu season or the onset of a cold. Tincturing preserves its immune-modulating properties, allowing for easy daily consumption.

- **Valerian:** Known for its sedative properties, Valerian root is a popular herb for those battling insomnia or anxiety. In tincture form, it can be taken before bedtime or during stressful periods to induce calm and improve sleep quality.
- **Milk Thistle:** This herb is highly valued for its liver-protective properties. Milk Thistle tinctures are often consumed by those looking to support liver health, especially after exposure to toxins or excessive alcohol consumption.
- **Ginkgo Biloba:** Ginkgo is heralded for its cognitive-enhancing effects. As a tincture, it is taken by many seeking to improve memory, focus, and overall brain function.
- **St. John's Wort:** A natural mood enhancer, St. John's Wort is often used as a remedy for mild to moderate depression. The tincture allows for easy dosage adjustments, making it convenient for daily consumption.

### Process

Chop the herb finely and place it in a jar. Cover with high-proof alcohol or vinegar, ensuring the herbs are completely submerged. Seal the jar and let it sit in a cool, dark place for several weeks, shaking occasionally. Afterward, strain out the herbs, leaving only the liquid, and store them in dark glass bottles.

## *Oils and Salves*

Herbal oils and salves stand as a testament to the versatility of plants in promoting health and well-being. While both are topical applications, they harness the healing power of herbs in slightly different ways. Oils involve the infusion of herbs in carrier oils to extract beneficial compounds, while salves take this a step further by thickening these oils with beeswax or other agents to create a semi-solid consistency. These preparations are especially beneficial for skin concerns, pain management, and more.

## Popular Herbs for Oils and Salves

Dive into some popular herbs used in oils and salves and their primary applications.

- **Calendula:** Known for its gentle, skin-soothing properties, calendula oil or salve is a staple in many natural skincare routines. It is beneficial for reducing inflammation, healing minor wounds, and soothing irritated skin.
- **Arnica:** Arnica is renowned for its pain-relieving properties. An arnica oil or salve is often applied to bruises, sprains, or sore muscles to reduce pain and swelling.
- **Lavender:** Besides its aromatic appeal, lavender-infused oil or salve possesses calming and antibacterial properties. It is excellent for minor burns and insect bites and promotes relaxation when massaged onto temples.
- **Comfrey:** Often referred to as *'knit-bone,'* comfrey is used in salves to support the healing of broken bones, sprains, and strains. Its allantoin content promotes cell growth, speeding up healing processes.

When crafting or selecting herbal oils and salves, ensuring that the herbs used are high quality and that the carrier oil is appropriate for the intended use is essential. For instance, coconut oil, with its natural antimicrobial properties, might be preferable for a wound-healing salve, while olive oil could be more suitable for general skin care.

### *Freezing*

In herbal preservation, freezing stands out as a method that locks in the vibrant color, aroma, and flavor of fresh herbs. While drying or tincturing often alters the herb's characteristics somewhat, freezing preserves the herb's fresh essence. Chefs and home cooks especially favor this technique, but it is also cherished by those who love making fresh herbal concoctions at home. Below is how the process works and spotlights some herbs well-suited for freezing.

#### How it Works

Freezing herbs essentially *"pauses"* the herb in its fresh state. As the water content in the herbs turns to ice, it prevents the growth of microorganisms that can cause decay or spoilage. When you are ready to use the herb, simply retrieve it from the freezer, and, in many cases, you can use it almost as you would a fresh herb. However, while the flavor remains, the texture of the herb might change after freezing, making it more suitable for cooked dishes or teas rather than as a fresh garnish.

#### Popular Herbs to Freeze:

Explore some of the best herbs to freeze below.

- **Basil:** Often used in Italian cuisine, frozen basil retains much of its rich, aromatic flavor. It can be incorporated into sauces, pestos, or soups.
- **Parsley:** Parsley is a versatile herb, and when frozen, it can be added to various dishes, from soups to casseroles, imparting its fresh, slightly peppery taste.
- **Cilantro (Coriander):** A staple in many Mexican and Asian dishes, frozen cilantro maintains its distinctive zesty and citrusy flavor profile, suitable for salsas, curries, and marinades.

- **Mint:** Mint, when frozen, remains refreshingly cool in flavor. It is excellent for brewing into teas, blending into smoothies, or adding to desserts.
- **Chives:** With a delicate onion flavor, frozen chives can be sprinkled over baked potatoes, folded into omelets, or incorporated into creamy dips.

### Tip for Freezing

When freezing herbs, one can either store them whole or chop them up and store them in ice cube trays with a bit of water or oil. This latter method allows for easy portioning when it is time to use. Regardless of the chosen technique, always ensure the herbs are clean and dry before freezing to maintain optimal quality.

## Dosages

In the universe of herbal remedies, simply knowing which herb to use is not enough. How you prepare that herb and the dosage you take are equally crucial. One might wonder, *"Is not it enough to just brew some tea with the herb and drink it?"* The reality, as you will soon discover, is far more nuanced. This section delves into the science and art of preparing herbs and determining the right dosages for optimal benefits.

### *Calculating Effective Dosages*

Every individual is unique, and so is their reaction to different herbs. What works wonders for one might not produce the same effects for another. Hence, understanding dosages is not just beneficial; it is essential. To help you with this, make sure to remember the tips below.

- **Starting Low:** For those new to herbal remedies, it is always wise to start with a lower dosage and observe how your body reacts. This minimizes potential side effects and helps you identify the right amount for your specific needs.

- **Factor in Age and Body Weight:** Children or individuals with lower body weights generally require smaller doses. It is a basic principle but one that is often overlooked.
- **Form of the Herb:** The potency of an herb can vary depending on its form. For instance, dried herbs might require a different dosage than tinctures or extracts. Always refer to guidelines specific to the form you are using.
- **Consistency is Key:** Herbal remedies often work best when taken consistently over time rather than in large, sporadic doses. Consistency aids in building the beneficial compounds in your system, leading to more pronounced effects.

## Combining Herbs for Synergy

In the vast world of nature, herbs are like individual musical notes. When played together, they can create a harmonious melody. But just as in music, mixing different notes—or, in this case, herbs—needs knowledge and care. Now, you will explore how to skillfully combine herbs for the best results.

### *Principles of Combining Herbs.*

Like chefs blend ingredients to create a perfect dish, herbalists mix herbs to achieve specific therapeutic outcomes. Before delving into the guidelines for combining herbs, it is essential to grasp some foundational principles. Here is what you need to know:

### Note Complementary Actions

Pairing herbs complementing each other's actions can lead to more comprehensive solutions. For instance, if one herb helps soothe the digestive system, another that aids digestion can be its perfect companion. This combination provides both relief and support to the digestive process.

### Avoid Overlaps

Ensuring you are not doubling up on the same properties, which might lead to excessive dosages, is essential. For example, combining two sedative herbs might result in excessive drowsiness or other potential side effects.

### Taste and Preparation Compatibility

Herbs also have unique flavors and preparation methods. Some herbs might be bitter, while others could be sweet or savory. Ensuring a harmonious taste can make the herbal remedy more palatable. Additionally, considering preparation methods ensures the combined herbs can be effectively brewed or mixed.

## *Exploring Classic Herb Combinations*

Across cultures and centuries, certain herbal combinations have become staples due to their enhanced efficacy when used together. These combinations are often more potent and beneficial than when each herb is used alone.

### Turmeric and Black Pepper

Hailing from the Ayurvedic tradition, turmeric is renowned for its anti-inflammatory benefits. But there is a catch: while turmeric contains a potent compound called curcumin, our bodies do not absorb it well. That is where black pepper comes into play. Black pepper contains piperine, which boosts the body's ability to absorb curcumin by a whopping 2000%. So, when you mix turmeric and black pepper, you are not just blending flavors but creating a powerful team for pain relief and immune support.

### Lavender and Chamomile

From the heart of European herbal traditions come lavender and chamomile, two herbs celebrated for their calming vibes. Both are go-to's for encouraging a peaceful night's sleep. Together, they supercharge each other, offering a synergistic punch that helps melt away stress and ushers in a deeper, more restful sleep.

### Ginseng and Ginkgo Biloba

Rooted in Traditional Chinese Medicine, Ginseng shines as a natural stress reducer and energy booster, while Ginkgo Biloba gets props for sharpening memory and cognition. When these two join forces, they create a dynamic duo that elevates mental clarity, increases focus, and brings a fresh burst of vitality.

### Milk Thistle and Dandelion

These two herbs are often paired up for their liver-loving qualities. Milk Thistle acts like a liver's bodyguard, shielding it from toxins and supporting its overall function. On the other hand, Dandelion steps in with its knack for boosting bile production and its diuretic touch, ensuring the liver gets a proper cleanse. When teamed up, they are like a detox dream team for your liver.

### Lemon Balm and Peppermint:

From the rich tapestry of European herbal tradition come Lemon Balm and Peppermint, two herbs with a soft spot for our digestive system. Lemon Balm, with its gentle touch, eases digestive discomfort and doubles as a nerve calmer. Meanwhile, Peppermint steps up to bat against the irritating symptoms of IBS and soothes indigestion. Put them together, and you have a refreshing, dynamic duo ready to tackle all tummy troubles.

## Safety in Using Herbs

While the world of herbs offers many remedies and benefits, it is essential to remember that not all plants are created equal. Some can be beneficial in small amounts but harmful in larger doses, while others might not mix well with certain medications.

### *Recognizing Toxic Plants*

Not all green is good. Nature, in its diverse forms, has plants that heal and those that harm. For every chamomile and lavender, plants with toxic properties can be harmful if ingested or even touched. To avoid being harmed, follow the tips below.

- **Educate Yourself:** Before foraging or consuming any wild plant, ensure you accurately identify it. Many beneficial plants have toxic look-alikes. For instance, the beneficial wild carrot closely resembles the harmful water hemlock.
- **Consult Field Guides:** Invest in a good field guide specific to your region. These guides provide clear photographs and descriptions, aiding accurate identification.
- **Attend Workshops:** Local herbalists or botanists often conduct workshops where you can learn to recognize both beneficial and toxic plants in your area.

### *Herb-Drug Interactions*

Herbs, though natural, have potent compounds that can interfere with synthetic drugs, either diminishing their effect, enhancing it, or producing unwanted side effects. Here are some tips to help you with this:

- **Maintain a List:** Always keep an updated list of all your medications and supplements. This will be handy if you consult a professional.
- **Consult Before Combining:** Before starting any herbal remedy, consult a healthcare provider or pharmacist about potential interactions.
- **Stay Updated:** New research is continually shedding light on potential interactions. Regularly updating your knowledge can help ensure safe usage. For example, St. John's Wort, a common herbal remedy for depression, can interfere with several medications, including birth control pills and antiretroviral drugs.

## *Allergies and Sensitivities*

Just as some people are allergic to certain foods or pollens, sensitivities can also arise with herbs. Recognizing and respecting these sensitivities is crucial. Listed below are tips for you to effectively address allergies and sensitivities.

- **Start Small:** If trying an herb for the first time, start with a small dose to observe any adverse reactions before committing to a regular dose.
- **Listen to Your Body:** Pay attention to any unusual symptoms after consuming an herb, such as itching, hives, swelling, or respiratory issues. These might be signs of an allergic reaction.
- **Skin Patch Test:** For topical herbal products, perform a patch test. Apply a small amount to a skin patch and wait 24 hours to check for reactions.
- **Know the Common Culprits:** Some herbs are more likely to cause allergic reactions than others. For example, chamomile and ragweed belong to the same family and can cross-react. If you are allergic to ragweed, you might also react to chamomile.

# CHAPTER 4

# Herbal Remedies for Common Ailments

Herbal remedies, utilized for centuries in traditional medicine systems across cultures, provide natural ways to address common health concerns. From respiratory issues to skincare, herbs can lend their healing properties to rejuvenate the body and restore balance. This comprehensive chapter explores how you can harness the potency of herbs to alleviate everyday ailments. It discusses herbal solutions for common digestive problems, respiratory conditions, and immunity boosting. You will also uncover herbs that can enhance the health and beauty of your skin and hair.

## Digestive and Gut Health

Digestive health is crucial for overall well-being and is pivotal in nutrient absorption, immune function, and more. *But what happens when your digestive system is out of balance?* This section discusses the importance of gut health, herbal remedies to address common digestive issues, the benefits of probiotic herbs, and understanding food sensitivities.

## *Herbs for Common Digestive Issues*

Digestive issues, while common, can greatly disrupt your daily routines and overall well-being. The modern diet, laden with processed foods and stressors, often affects your digestive system. However, in its immense bounty, nature has provided a range of herbs that alleviate symptoms and nurture the digestive process. Here are some of these herbal wonders.

### Ginger

This spicy, fragrant root has been a staple in traditional medicine for millennia, cherished for its potent digestive and anti-inflammatory properties. It is known for combatting nausea. Whether it is motion sickness, pregnancy-induced nausea, or post-operative unease, ginger can offer relief. Its compounds, especially gingerol, help regulate digestive movements and soothe the stomach. Ginger can also stimulate digestive enzymes, ensuring efficient breakdown and absorption of nutrients. Thereby improving digestion.

***Tip:*** *On a turbulent flight or a sea voyage, carrying some ginger candies or sipping ginger tea can be a game-changer, ensuring a smoother journey.*

### Peppermint

Beyond its refreshing taste, peppermint houses a wealth of health benefits, especially for the digestive tract. It can soothe IBS symptoms. Studies have shown that peppermint oil can alleviate the spasms and discomfort associated with irritable bowel syndrome (IBS). Its antispasmodic properties help relax the muscles of the gastrointestinal tract. Also, the cooling sensation of peppermint can help ease indigestion and discomfort after a rich meal. Think of peppermint as a gentle breeze on a hot day, offering relief and comfort to an overworked digestive system.

### Fennel

This aromatic herb, with its licorice-like flavor, is more than just a culinary delight. Fennel seeds contain compounds that reduce gas production and help expel it, thus preventing bloating and that uncomfortable *"full"* feeling. It can also be considered a digestive stimulant, as fennel can stimulate the production of gastric juices, facilitating a smoother digestive process.

## *Probiotic Herbs*

The word *"probiotic"* often brings images of yogurt containers or supplement pills promising to boost gut health. But nature, in its vast wisdom, has provided us with herbal allies that can support the digestive system. These probiotic herbs help balance gut flora and offer additional health benefits, making them an essential tool for those seeking natural ways to enhance digestive health.

### Dandelion

Dandelion, often dismissed as a mere garden intruder, is brimming with health benefits. Its roots are rich in inulin, a soluble fiber that acts as a prebiotic, nourishing the beneficial bacteria in the gut. As these bacteria consume inulin, they increase and foster a harmonious gut environment. Moreover, dandelion aids digestion by stimulating bile production, which is especially beneficial after consuming fatty meals. Think of dandelion as the dedicated guardian of your internal garden, ensuring fertile ground where beneficial bacteria can thrive.

### Marshmallow Root

Marshmallow root, while not a probiotic herb in the traditional sense, plays a pivotal role in gut health. Rich in mucilage, a gelatinous substance, it imparts a soothing effect on the gut lining, acting as a protective shield that is especially beneficial for those with sensitive or inflamed digestive systems. This root alleviates inflammation and irritation and ensures the gut remains a conducive sanctuary for probiotic bacteria. Picture marshmallow root as the steadfast sentinel of a fortress, reinforcing its walls and preserving a serene and hospitable environment within for its inhabitants.

### Burdock Root

Burdock root, with its distinct earthy flavor, is an unsung hero among herbs. Celebrated historically for its potent detoxifying abilities, it aids the body in flushing out toxins, ensuring they do not accumulate and precipitate health complications. Additionally, akin to dandelion, burdock root is a treasure trove of inulin, which supports a thriving environment for probiotic bacteria in the gut.

## *Addressing Food Sensitivities*

Food sensitivities can subtly disrupt your daily life, manifesting as persistent digestive discomfort, fatigue, or mood swings. Unlike food allergies, which can trigger immediate and severe reactions, food sensitivities are often more elusive, leading to chronic symptoms over time. Recognizing and addressing these sensitivities improves digestive health and enhances overall well-being. To do so, follow the steps below.

### Identifying the Culprit

Before you can address a problem, you need to identify it. The first step in pinpointing food sensitivities is being observant.

- **Food Diary:** Maintaining a detailed food diary is pivotal. For a few weeks, jot down everything you eat and drink, no matter how insignificant it may seem. Alongside this, note any symptoms you experience – bloating, headaches, fatigue, or mood swings.

- **Detect Patterns:** As days turn into weeks, you may begin to see patterns. Perhaps that recurring headache always happens a couple of hours after eating dairy. Or maybe the bloating is most pronounced on days you consume gluten. These patterns can offer invaluable clues.

## Elimination Diet

Once you have a hunch about a particular food or group of foods, the elimination diet can provide clearer answers. Remove the suspected food or foods from your diet entirely for a set period, typically 3 to 4 weeks. It is crucial to be thorough—even trace amounts can trigger symptoms in sensitive individuals.

During this period, continue noting any symptoms in your food diary. Many people experience a noticeable improvement in their symptoms, suggesting a potential sensitivity.

## Reintroduction

Reintroducing the food is as important as eliminating it. This step helps confirm whether the food was genuinely the source of your discomfort or a coincidence.

After the elimination phase, reintroduce the suspected food gradually. Start with a small amount and observe any reactions. If there are none, increase the quantity over a few days.

If symptoms reappear upon reintroduction, it is a strong indication of sensitivity. However, if there are no adverse reactions, the initial symptoms might have been coincidental, or the sensitivity could be dose-dependent, meaning it only manifests after a certain amount is consumed.

## Respiratory and Immune Health

The respiratory and immune systems act as the primary defenders against environmental aggressors. These systems tirelessly work to keep us healthy, from the air we breathe to the pathogens we unknowingly encounter. *But what if you could bolster these natural defenses?*

### *Herbs for Common Respiratory Issues*

Each breath you take showcases your body's remarkable ability to persevere, thanks to the relentless work of the lungs. Yet, even the most efficient systems can face setbacks. Respiratory issues can be unsettling, whether it is a persistent cough or a weighty feeling in the chest. These respiratory challenges, though common, need not always be tackled with over-the-counter drugs. Sometimes, the remedy lies in your backyard or garden. Embracing the potency of the herbs below means aligning oneself with nature's rhythm, ensuring each breath is deep, clear, and full of life.

#### Eucalyptus

Eucalyptus, often recognized for its refreshing scent, provides benefits beyond its aromatic allure. The oil derived from this towering tree is a natural decongestant, lending itself to steams or rubs that facilitate deeper, unobstructed breathing. Moreover, the inherent antibacterial properties of eucalyptus aid in combating respiratory infections, potentially diminishing both their duration and severity. For those seeking quick relief, adding a few drops of eucalyptus oil to a bowl of hot water and inhaling deeply can help clear the airways effectively.

## Mullein

Mullein, characterized by its velvety leaves and towering spikes of golden-yellow flowers, is nature's comforting remedy for the respiratory system. Particularly effective for alleviating dry, hacking coughs, mullein offers gentle relief by coating the throat and minimizing irritation. Additionally, when consumed, it supports the bronchial tubes by decreasing inflammation, paving the way for more effortless breathing. A simple yet therapeutic way to harness its benefits is by steeping dried mullein leaves in hot water to prepare a rejuvenating tea. For a delightful taste and added healing properties, a spoonful of honey can be a perfect complement.

## Thyme

Thyme, commonly found among kitchen spices, offers more than just culinary allure; it is packed with medicinal potency. Beyond its ability to flavor dishes, thyme's antispasmodic attributes provide solace from persistent coughs, aiding in uninterrupted, peaceful nights. Moreover, the herb's inherent antibacterial and antifungal properties equip the body to fend off respiratory infections, strengthening its natural defenses. A practical and tasty way to harness thyme's benefits is by blending its leaves with honey. This fusion not only results in a delightful spread for toasts but, when ingested directly, also doubles as an efficacious remedy.

## Licorice Root

Licorice root, often recognized for its association with candy flavors, extends its benefits beyond just a sweet taste. This herb plays a pivotal role in respiratory wellness. Its anti-inflammatory properties can soothe symptoms such as sore throats and chest tightness. Additionally, licorice root serves as an expectorant, aiding in the loosening and expulsion of mucus, thereby facilitating clearer airways. For those seeking a tangible way to embrace its benefits, brewing a warm cup of licorice root tea can be an ideal and comforting choice, particularly on chilly winter nights.

## *Boosting Immunity Naturally*

In the intricate workings of the body, the immune system stands as a vigilant guard, always on the lookout for potential threats. Yet, even the strongest guards can use some reinforcement. Delving into the world of plants and herbs, you will find nature's warriors. These herbs, celebrated across different cultures and times, offer their strength to bolster your immune defenses.

### Echinacea

Echinacea, a garden beauty, boasts health benefits as striking as its appearance. Not only does it act as an immune modulator, adjusting the immune system's response up or down depending on the need, but it also has potent anti-inflammatory properties. These qualities ensure the body's defenses remain balanced, preventing excessive reactions that can lead to problems like autoimmune responses. For those feeling the beginning twinges of a cold or flu, a timely cup of echinacea tea can help lessen both the severity and duration of the symptoms.

### Astragalus

Astragalus, an ancient root with enduring relevance, is a trusted pillar in traditional healing rituals. It boasts adaptogenic properties, enabling the body to resiliently navigate diverse stressors, whether physical, mental, or environmental. A body fortified by Astragalus is more adept at warding off sickness. Furthermore, astragalus improves the body's defense by enhancing the production of white blood cells, the body's primary warriors against microbial threats. For those looking to integrate this herb into their diets, adding slices of astragalus root to soups or broths introduces a subtle, sweet undertone and gifts the dish with an immunity-enhancing touch.

## Elderberry

Elderberries, with their dark and glossy appearance, are diminutive powerhouses for bolstering immune defenses. Renowned for their ability to hinder viral replication, they are pivotal in curtailing infections aiding in quicker recovery. A generous vitamin C content, a robust antioxidant, further enriches their potency. This vitamin supports diverse cellular functions within the immune system and acts as a frontline shield. For those keen on incorporating elderberries into their regimen, a dose of elderberry syrup at the initial hints of illness can prove transformative. And for a delightful morning twist, consider drizzling it over pancakes, merging flavor with health benefits.

## Turmeric

Bright and resplendent in its golden hue, turmeric transcends its culinary role in the kitchen. Renowned as a potent immunomodulatory agent, it owes much of its prowess to curcumin, its active compound. With pronounced anti-inflammatory and antioxidant attributes, curcumin underpins turmeric's immense contributions to immune vitality. Furthermore, turmeric's ability to amplify the body's antibody response refines its proficiency in neutralizing external threats. Consider indulging in a golden milk latte for those exploring ways to incorporate this wonder herb into their daily routine. Crafted by simmering turmeric in milk and adding a hint of black pepper to bolster absorption, this beverage is a treat to the palate and a fortifying elixir for health.

## *Herbs for Seasonal Allergy Relief*

The beauty of blooming flowers and the melody of chirping birds often herald the arrival of spring. However, for many, this also signifies the onset of pesky seasonal allergies. *The silver lining?* In its benevolence, nature provides not just the triggers but also the remedies. Dive into the herbal solutions that can offer a reprieve from the sneezing, itching, and general discomfort of allergies.

### Nettle

Often evoking apprehension due to its stinging touch, the nettle plant harbors a paradox within its leaves—an antidote for allergic reactions. Renowned as a natural antihistamine, nettle offers relief from common allergic manifestations such as sneezing, nasal congestion, and the incessant itchiness of the eyes. But the plant's offerings do not just stop at allergies. Its intrinsic anti-inflammatory virtues extend to benefit overall respiratory health. A cup of nettle tea, especially during pollen-heavy periods, can be a strategic shield for those grappling with seasonal allergies. However, the market is replete with nettle supplements for those less inclined towards teas, presenting an alternative route to harness its benefits.

### Butterbur

characterized by its expansive, shield-like leaves, mirrors its physical trait in function by acting as a protective barrier against allergies. It suppresses leukotrienes and histamines, the culprits behind most allergy symptoms. Clinical research touts butterbur's efficacy, placing it on par with many over-the-counter antihistamines but with the distinct advantage of not inducing drowsiness. For those looking to use this herb, butterbur extracts are available in capsule and tincture forms. A word of caution: always prioritize products labeled as *"PA-free,"* ensuring they are free from potentially harmful alkaloids.

### Eyebright

Eyebright, with its delicate white and purple flowers, is much more than just a visual delight. As the name suggests, this herb has been an age-old remedy for eye-related ailments. When allergies strike, leading to itchy, red, and watery eyes, eyebright comes to the rescue with its anti-inflammatory properties. Its natural compounds help soothe eye tissues and reduce inflammation, making it an ideal herbal remedy during allergy seasons, where pollen can irritate the eyes.

### Golden Herb

Goldenseal, a perennial herb native to the eastern United States, is a powerhouse in herbal medicine. Traditionally, it has been prized for its antibiotic and immune-boosting properties. One of the standout benefits for allergy sufferers is its astringent properties, derived primarily from its active compound berberine. This property can help reduce excessive mucous production and watery discharge often seen in allergic reactions, making it particularly useful during high pollen seasons when runny noses are prevalent.

## Skin and Hair Care

The skin and hair are the crowning glory of a person's physical appearance. They not only add to your beauty but also indicate your overall health. As it is the body's first line of defense, the skin is constantly exposed to various elements, while the hair faces its share of challenges. Just as plants and herbs thrive in the right environment, so do skin and hair with the right care. Dive into nature's trove to discover herbal remedies for common beauty concerns.

## *Herbs for Common Skin Issues*

The skin, a protective barrier, is often the first to manifest internal imbalances or external stressors. Before reaching for chemical-laden creams, consider the soothing embrace of herbs.

### Aloe Vera

Aloe Vera, often dubbed the *"wonder plant,"* possesses succulent leaves packed with a gel that is nothing short of a miracle elixir for many skin concerns. Predominantly recognized for its cooling properties, Aloe Vera emerges as a frontline remedy for sunburns, providing immediate relief and accelerating healing. But the benefits do not just stop at burns. The gel is a natural moisturizer that deeply hydrates the skin, addressing dryness and flakiness. What is particularly impressive about Aloe Vera is its ability to moisturize without imparting a greasy residue, making it an ideal choice for all skin types, from the driest to the oiliest. Whether applied directly from the leaf or used in formulated skincare products, aloe vera is an indispensable ally in maintaining skin health and radiance.

### Calendula

Calendula, with its vibrant golden petals, offers more than just visual delight. Beyond its aesthetic charm, this botanical wonder is a powerhouse when it comes to skin health. Renowned for its anti-inflammatory properties, calendula excels at soothing various skin irritations, ranging from redness and itchiness to more severe inflammations like eczema or rosacea. Its calming effects on the skin make it a go-to choice for those with sensitive or reactive skin types. Additionally, the herb's potent healing attributes are invaluable in the swift recovery of minor cuts, scrapes, or wounds. The magic of calendula can be harnessed in various forms, including infused oils, balms, or creams. Integrating calendula-based products into your skincare routine can be a transformative step towards achieving supple, resilient, and blemish-free skin.

### Chamomile

Chamomile, often cherished as a calming tea, holds a lesser-known secret: it is a powerhouse for skin care. Especially beneficial for sensitive skin, chamomile has the innate ability to soothe redness and irritation, rendering it a balm for those who grapple with skin flare-ups. Its gentle nature makes it a go-to for people with reactive skin, helping to maintain a calm and balanced complexion. Moreover, for those battling the pesky acne issue, chamomile brings to the table its antiseptic properties, which reduce current flare-ups and prevent future ones. It operates with the body's natural healing processes, promoting clearer, healthier skin.

## *Natural Hair Care Solutions*

Healthy and shiny hair is a sign of good health and vitality. However, factors like pollution and stress from modern life can take a toll on your hair's condition. Uncover nature's solutions to common hair problems below.

### Rosemary

Rosemary, a fragrant herb commonly used in cooking, also offers remarkable benefits for hair. It strengthens hair from its roots, reducing breakage and thinning. Furthermore, if your hair has lost its shine, rosemary can restore its natural luster. To harness these benefits, consider using rosemary-infused oils or shampoos. Regular scalp massages with rosemary oil can enhance hair health and even improve scalp blood circulation. Over time, consistent use can lead to stronger, shinier hair.

### Hibiscus

Hibiscus, with its vibrant blooms commonly seen in tropical gardens, is an ornamental delight and a powerful ally in hair care. The petals and leaves of the hibiscus plant are rich in nutrients that fortify hair strands, making them resistant to breakage, thus reducing hair fall. Additionally, the natural mucilage in hibiscus acts as a conditioner, leaving hair feeling soft, manageable, and silky. Just as plants flourish with proper nutrition, the hair blossoms when provided with the right care. Using hibiscus-infused treatments or oils can be as rejuvenating for the hair as a refreshing spell of rain is for thirsty plants. Consider incorporating hibiscus-based hair masks or rinses into your hair care routine for healthier, more radiant locks.

## *Herbal Beauty and Anti-Aging Treatments*

Aging is a natural process, but premature aging is not. Harness the power of herbs to retain that youthful glow and delay the appearance of age-related signs.

### Ginseng

Ginseng, deeply revered in Asian medicine for centuries, is not only a potent adaptogen but also a powerhouse when it comes to anti-aging skin benefits. At the heart of skin's elasticity and firmness is collagen, a protein that naturally decreases with age. Ginseng steps in by promoting collagen production, effectively reducing the appearance of fine lines and wrinkles that are indicative of aging skin. But its benefits do not stop there. The myriad of nutrients and antioxidants in ginseng can work wonders on age spots, evening out skin tone and bestowing a radiant, youthful glow to the complexion. This dynamic root does not just address aging on the surface; it delves deep, revitalizing skin cells and enhancing overall skin health. Once you incorporate ginseng-infused products into one's skincare routine, you are investing in a time-tested ingredient that has been cherished for its age-defying properties for generations.

## Lavender

When it comes to skin, especially aging skin, lavender emerges as a rejuvenating herb. One of its most prized benefits is its ability to hydrate the skin deeply, which in turn helps diminish the appearance of wrinkles. Over time, as the skin naturally loses its elasticity and becomes more sensitive, lavender becomes a healer. It is particularly effective in addressing age-related skin sensitivities, soothing the skin, and promoting a youthful glow. So, while it might be known for its calming scent, lavender's gifts to the realm of anti-aging are undeniably significant.

# Chapter 5

# Herbalism for Family and Pets

In this chapter, you will begin by exploring common herbal solutions for various childhood ailments. With a focus on safety and proper dosing, you will learn how to gently treat colds, stomach upsets, skin issues, and more using natural botanicals. Insights are also provided on boosting children's immunity and overall well-being. The next section delves into women's herbal health, providing remedies to navigate life's transitions from puberty to menopause. You will discover herbs that support menstrual health, fertility, pregnancy, and graceful aging. Finally, the use of herbs for pets is covered, outlining their benefits for common pet ailments, enhancing longevity, and integrating into a holistic wellness routine.

## Herbal Remedies for Children

In this day and age, where conventional medicine is within easy reach, many parents are looking to nature for gentler solutions to common childhood ailments. This section will introduce you to herbal remedies specifically tailored for children.

## *Common Childhood Ailments*

Children, with their growing bodies and evolving immune systems, are often prone to specific health concerns. Thankfully, nature provides a bounty of herbs to help in these situations. Here are some of the common health issues children experience and natural solutions to use for them.

- **Colds and Flu:** Probably the most common of childhood ailments. Rather than reaching for over-the-counter medications, consider Echinacea. This purple coneflower has been a favorite for generations to shorten the duration of colds and boost the immune system. Another helpful herb is Elderberry, which is often consumed as a syrup and has antiviral properties that combat the flu.
- **Stomach Upsets:** Chamomile is a go-to remedy for digestive discomforts. This gentle herb soothes the stomach and can also help with sleep. For children with gas, fennel seeds brewed into a tea can offer relief.
- **Skin Rashes and Eczema:** Calendula, often found in creams and lotions, is a potent healer for skin issues. Its anti-inflammatory properties can soothe irritated skin and promote healing.
- **Toothaches and Gum Issues:** Clove oil has been a natural remedy for dental pains for centuries. Its antiseptic and analgesic properties can help numb the pain and fight against bacteria. However, it should be used sparingly and never directly on the gums. Instead, dilute a drop in a teaspoon of carrier oil and apply using a cotton ball.
- **Ear Infections:** Mullein garlic oil can be a soothing remedy for earaches often caused by infections. While garlic has antibacterial properties, mullein acts as a pain reliever. Warm the oil slightly (always test the temperature first to ensure it is lukewarm, not hot), and put a couple of drops into the affected ear. Remember, this remedy is only for

non-punctured eardrums. If any doubt or symptoms persist, always consult a healthcare provider.

- **Restlessness and Sleep Issues:** Lemon balm is an excellent herb for calming a restless child. It has mild sedative properties, aiding relaxation and promoting sleep. You can brew it into a tea or offer it as a tincture in reduced dosages, suitable for children.
- **Cuts and Scrapes:** Plantain, commonly regarded as a weed in many gardens, is a gem for minor skin injuries. The crushed fresh leaves of plantain can be applied directly to small wounds to promote healing and reduce the risk of infection due to its antibacterial properties.
- **Allergies and Hay Fever:** Butterbur has shown promise in treating hay fever symptoms without the drowsiness that typical antihistamines might cause. Its extracts can reduce sneezing, itchy eyes, and other allergy symptoms. Ensure that the product you are using is labeled *'PA-free,'* which means it does not contain liver-toxic pyrrolizidine alkaloids.

## *Dosage and Safety Considerations*

While herbal remedies can be effective, you must remember that children's bodies are not just miniature versions of adults. They metabolize and react differently to substances, so special attention should be paid to dosages and safety. Here are some tips you can use when using herbal remedies for children.

- **Start Low, Go Slow:** Always introduce a new herbal remedy in a small dose to observe how your child reacts. If no adverse effects are noticed, you can gradually increase the recommended dose.
- **Consult Professionals:** Before introducing any herbal treatment, especially if your child is on other medications, consult a pediatrician or a professional herbalist.

- **Choose Quality Products:** Ensure that you are sourcing herbs from reputable suppliers. Look for organic, non-GMO products free from pesticides and other contaminants.
- **Understand the Child's Age and Weight:** One of the essential factors when administering herbal remedies is to consider the child's age and weight. Dosages that may be suitable for a teenager would undoubtedly be too much for a toddler. For instance, while an adult might take a teaspoon of a certain tincture, a younger child might only need a few drops.
- **Topical vs. Internal Use:** Some herbs are more suitable for topical application, while others can be consumed. Parents should be clear about the method of use. For example, while chamomile can be ingested as a tea or given in small amounts as a tincture, calendula is more commonly used as a cream or ointment for skin irritations. Always ensure that any product meant for topical use is kept out of the reach of children to avoid accidental ingestion.
- **Avoid Potential Allergens:** Children can be allergic to certain herbs, just like foods. When introducing a new herbal remedy, parents should always monitor their kids for allergic reactions. Signs might include skin rashes, difficulty breathing, or an upset stomach. If these symptoms appear, discontinue use immediately and consult a healthcare professional.
- **Storage and Shelf Life:** Just like conventional medicines, herbal remedies have an expiration date. Parents should ensure they store all herbal products in a cool, dry place, away from direct sunlight. Keeping them out of the reach of children is vital to prevent accidental misuse. Regularly check for any changes in smell, color, or texture, as this could indicate the product is no longer suitable for use.
- **Educate and Involve Your Child:** It is a good practice to educate kids about the herbal remedies they are taking. Discuss with them the benefits and reasons for

taking the herbs. As they grow older, they can become more involved in understanding their health and the natural ways to maintain it. This can also cultivate a sense of respect and appreciation for nature's gifts.

### *Boosting Immunity and Wellness*

Beyond treating ailments, herbs can be powerful allies in maintaining wellness and boosting immunity, ensuring children remain healthy and resilient. Children's health is an ever-evolving landscape, and as parents seek out the best for their little ones, having a wider arsenal of natural tools is helpful. Here, you will explore more herbs that have been cherished for their benefit to children.

- **Astragalus Root:** This herb, commonly used in traditional Chinese medicine, increases the body's resistance to stress and diseases. It is a great tonic for enhancing overall immunity.
- **Cod Liver Oil:** While not a herb, cod liver oil is packed with omega-3 fatty acids and vitamins A and D, crucial for bone health, brain development, and immunity.
- **Nettle Leaf:** An excellent source of vitamins and minerals, nettle leaf can be brewed into tea or even added to foods. It supports overall health and vitality.
- **Gotu Kola:** This herb is believed to support cognitive function. For children struggling with focus in school, a mild tea or tincture of gotu kola can be a natural way to enhance attention span, of course, with the guidance of an herbalist.
- **Peppermint:** Beyond the delightful taste, peppermint can soothe an upset tummy. Cold peppermint tea can be a refreshing and calming drink for kids experiencing nausea or digestive discomfort.

- **Horsetail:** This ancient plant is a natural source of silica, which plays a crucial role in building and maintaining healthy bones and teeth. It can be infused with water and consumed as tea.

## Women's Herbal Health through Life's Stages

As a woman journeys through the different seasons of her life, her body experiences diverse changes that are both empowering and challenging. Nature, with its rich tapestry of herbs, offers holistic solutions to these transitions, ensuring wellness at every phase. In this section, you will see the profound relationship between women and the botanical world as it gracefully supports them from pregnancy to aging.

### *Pregnancy and Postpartum*

Pregnancy is often likened to a rollercoaster ride filled with exhilarating highs and daunting challenges. From the first flutter in the belly to the intense labor pains, it is a transformative journey. The body expands, hormones dance in new rhythms, and emotions oscillate, ranging from overwhelming joy to heightened anxiety.

Postpartum, on the other hand, is the gentle descent from this rollercoaster. While it brings the unparalleled joy of cradling one's baby, it also presents challenges such as hormonal shifts, postpartum blues, and the pressures of new motherhood. Sleepless nights, breastfeeding woes, and dealing with the physical after-effects of birth can sometimes leave a new mother feeling depleted. During these profound transitions, nature steps in, offering herbal remedies that nurture and support.

Some recommended herbs are listed below.

- **Red Raspberry Leaf:** Known for its uterine-toning properties, red raspberry leaf is often visualized as nature's gentle hand guiding a woman through labor. Consumed as tea, this herb not only prepares the uterus for birth but also aids in faster recovery, helping mothers to rebound in the postpartum phase.
- **Nettle:** Imagine a herb that envelops the expectant mother and her growing fetus in a blanket of nutrients. That is nettle for you. High in essential minerals and vitamins, nettle tea is like a liquid embrace for the body, fortifying it during the demands of pregnancy.
- **Chamomile:** The postpartum phase can sometimes feel like walking through a fog of emotions. The highs of holding one's baby are occasionally interspersed with moments of anxiety and overwhelming feelings. Here, chamomile acts as a soft light, guiding the way. This gentle herb, consumed as tea, soothes the mind, eases emotional upheavals, and helps acquire restful sleep.

As magical as these herbs sound, it is paramount to remember that everybody is unique. Pregnancy and postpartum are deeply personal and sensitive periods. Just as you would be selective about the baby products you choose, be discerning about the herbs you consume. Always consult with a healthcare provider to ensure the safest journey for you and your little one.

### *Menstrual Health and Menopause*

From the tender teenage years marked by the onset of menstruation to the poignant phase of menopause, each stage has its unique challenges and experiences. While conventional medicines offer solutions, they sometimes have side effects that feel like trading one issue for another.

What makes herbal remedies more appealing for menstrual health is their gentle approach. Unlike synthetic medications, which can sometimes bulldoze their way through, causing side effects, herbs work synergistically with the body. They bolster the body's innate healing mechanisms without disrupting its natural balance. For instance, when dealing with hormonal fluctuations, herbs not only introduce external hormones but assist the body in producing and regulating its own, ensuring long-term health and balance. However, every woman's body tells a unique story, and what works for one may not work for another. But below, you will find the most common herbs for menstrual health and menopause.

- **Cramp Bark:** This remedy's name hints at its primary benefit: alleviating menstrual cramps. Cramp Bark, when consumed, acts like a soothing massage for the uterus. Its properties help relax those tight, spasming muscles, immediately relieving discomfort.
- **Vitex (Chasteberry):** Hormonal imbalances can sometimes feel like being on a boat in stormy seas. Vitex is like the anchor, helping to stabilize these hormonal waves. Promoting hormonal balance aids in addressing concerns like irregular cycles and intense PMS symptoms.
- **Black Cohosh:** This herb is beneficial in reducing menopause symptoms, particularly hot flashes. Hot flashes are sudden, temporary surges of heat that can cause sweating and discomfort. Black Cohosh aids in making the menopausal transition smoother by alleviating these symptoms.

## *Herbs for Bone Health and Aging Gracefully*

Aging is an art. While it is a natural progression of life, how you age can be a testament to your approach towards health and well-being. Particularly for women, the post-menopausal period can pose unique challenges, notably in bone health and cognitive function. However, numerous herbs offer support, ensuring the golden years are truly golden.

There is a certain elegance in turning to nature as one grows older. Nature moves in cycles; understanding these cycles can be the key to aging with grace. Herbs, in this respect, are not only curatives; they are partners, accompanying women through the transitions, ensuring vitality both in body and spirit.

- **Horsetail:** Horsetail offers resilience to the bones. Its high silica content is a building block, ensuring bones remain strong and less susceptible to fractures.
- **Red Clover:** Red clover, with its isoflavones, not only supports bone structure but also offers cardiovascular benefits. It is a reminder that holistic health is interconnected, where the health of one system can impact another.
- **Ginkgo Biloba:** Aging gracefully is not just about the body but also the mind. Ginkgo Biloba is known for enhancing memory and cognitive abilities, helping to keep memories sharp and clear throughout life.
- **Turmeric:** An age-old remedy, turmeric is renowned for its anti-inflammatory properties. As joint pains and inflammation can be concerns in advancing years, introducing turmeric into the diet can provide relief and mobility, allowing one to dance through the ages.

As you sail through the waters of time, remember that aging is about adding years to life and life to years. While herbs offer a gentle nudge, embracing a holistic lifestyle filled with joy, laughter, balanced nutrition, and movement can paint a masterpiece of your golden years.

## Herbal Care for Pets

Pets, like humans, often benefit from natural remedies. As interest in these for humans grows, so does the exploration of herbal solutions for our four-legged friends. Here, you will learn how herbal care can support pets in different stages of their life. From addressing ailments to ensuring a healthy, long life for our pets, this section will provide a comprehensive look into herbal pet care.

## *Why Introduce Pets to Herbs?*

Herbs have been a cornerstone of human wellness for millennia. But it is not just humans who can benefit from nature's pharmacy. Our furry companions—*particularly cats and dogs*— can thrive with the right herbal interventions.

The movement towards natural and holistic health is not limited to humans. Pets, as integral members of many families, are also being introduced to the world of herbal remedies. *But why the shift? What makes herbs an appealing avenue for pet wellness?*

- **Chemical-Free Living:** In a world where people continually question the side effects and long-term impact of synthetic medications, herbal treatments offer a more organic solution. They are free from synthetic chemicals and often have fewer side effects than conventional medications.
- **Harnessing Nature's Power:** Nature has been mankind's pharmacy for millennia, offering solutions for various ailments. Our pets, wild at their core, also have a natural affinity for certain herbs. They instinctively know, for example, to munch on specific grasses when they have a stomach upset. By introducing them to the right herbs, you align them closer to their natural tendencies.
- **Cost-Effective:** While some veterinary treatments can be expensive, many herbs can be grown in your backyard or sourced locally.
- **Prevention is Better than Cure:** Many herbs are known for their preventive qualities. Introducing pets to specific herbs can boost their immunity, reduce the risk of certain diseases, and improve overall vitality.

- **Holistic Wellness:** Herbs do not just address symptoms; they often target the root cause. For instance, rather than just suppressing a symptom like inflammation, herbs like turmeric address the underlying causes, promoting overall well-being.

## *Addressing Common Pet Ailments Naturally*

Like their human counterparts, pets too, encounter various health challenges. Instead of rushing to synthetic medications, certain herbal remedies can provide a natural alternative.

- **Digestive Issues:** Ginger can be a wonderful remedy for pets with motion sickness or general nausea. A tiny amount can ease their discomfort.
- **Joint Pain:** Turmeric, with its anti-inflammatory properties, can be beneficial for older pets experiencing arthritis or joint pains.
- **Skin Conditions:** Aloe Vera is a versatile plant that can soothe various skin conditions, from irritations to minor burns.
- **Anxiety:** Lavender, with its calming scent, can be used as essential oil (diluted) or dried flowers to ease anxiety, especially during thunderstorms or fireworks.
- **Respiratory Problems:** Mullein leaves can be a natural remedy for such challenges. When prepared as tea and mixed into their food, it can aid in clearing mucus from the respiratory tract.
- **Flea and Tick Prevention:** Nobody likes the idea of their beloved pets being bothered by pests like fleas and ticks. Rosemary can act as a natural deterrent. A rinse made from rosemary-infused water can help repel these pesky critters.
- **Boosting Immunity:** Echinacea, commonly associated with boosting human immune systems, can also benefit

pets. It can be given to pets recovering from illness to boost their immunity and speed up healing.

- **Urinary Tract Health:** Cranberries are not just for humans! When given appropriately, cranberry extract can promote urinary tract health in pets, helping prevent and treat infections.

Opting for natural remedies does not mean sidelining traditional veterinary care. It is essential to strike a balance. Always ensure that any herbal remedy introduced does not interfere with ongoing treatments and is suitable for your pet's needs.

### *Enhancing Pet Wellness and Longevity*

Anyone with a pet understands the depth of the bond that forms. They are not just animals; they are members of our family, partners in our daily lives, and sources of endless joy and love. The pain that comes from losing a pet is indescribable. It is a heartache that eventually eases with time but never truly goes away. This underscores the importance of enhancing their wellness and longevity. Every extra day, month, or year you get with your pet is precious, making pursuing their prolonged health and happiness worth every effort.

Embracing natural and herbal remedies is about giving pets the best possible life. Through the judicious use of these gifts from nature, combined with regular veterinary care, we ensure a holistic approach to their health. As stewards of their well-being, it is our duty to explore all avenues that lead to their happiness and longevity.

Remember, promoting pets' overall well-being is more than just addressing ailments. It also ensures they have a vibrant life filled with energy, playfulness, and longevity. Herbs can play a pivotal role in enhancing their overall wellness.

- **Dietary Supplements:** Flaxseeds, rich in Omega-3 fatty acids, can be added to your pet's diet to promote a shiny coat and healthy skin. They also support heart health.
- **Mental Stimulation:** Gotu Kola, often associated with cognitive benefits in humans, can also be given to pets in small amounts to enhance their memory and provide mental stimulation.
- **Detoxification:** Burdock root is a natural detoxifier for pets, helping eliminate toxins from the body and promoting better digestion and skin health.
- **Heart Health:** Hawthorn is an excellent herb for cardiovascular health. It strengthens and tones the heart muscles and can benefit older pets.
- **Nutritional Boost:** Spirulina, a blue-green algae, is packed with nutrients. Adding a pinch to your pet's food can ensure they get essential vitamins and minerals.
- **Dental Health:** Parsley is not just a garnish. Chewing on parsley can freshen your pet's breath and support dental health.
- **Heart Health:** Hawthorn berry supports cardiovascular health, ensuring your pet's heart remains strong and vital.
- **Immunity:** Echinacea, known for its immune-boosting properties, can be given during flu season or when there is a higher risk of infection.
- **Antioxidant Support:** Rosemary, an excellent natural flea repellent, also contains antioxidants. These help combat free radicals in the body, reducing the risk of chronic diseases and boosting overall health.
- **Liver Support:** Milk thistle is not just for humans. Given in controlled amounts, it can help detoxify your pet's liver, especially if they have been on medication.
- **Joint Mobility:** As pets age, their joints can become less flexible. Incorporating green-lipped mussels into their diet can provide natural glucosamine and chondroitin, supporting joint health and mobility.

# Chapter 6

# Herbalism in Daily Life

From infusing your favorite dishes with aromatic herbs to creating soothing herbal remedies, this chapter provides actionable tips to make herbalism an accessible and rewarding part of daily living. You will learn simple recipes to cook with herbs, make herbal beverages, set up an indoor herb garden, and harness the power of aromatics. With this wisdom, you can bridge the gap between ancient herbal traditions and modern lifestyle needs. Using herbs is a gentle way to nourish the body, awaken the senses, and cultivate a deeper connection with nature's healing gifts.

## Cooking with Herbs

Herbs have been an integral part of culinary traditions for millennia. But beyond their taste-enhancing properties, many herbs also bring many medicinal benefits. By incorporating them into your daily meals, you get to savor their flavors and reap their health rewards. In this section, you will dive right into the fascinating world of cooking with herbs, how you can infuse them into your dishes, craft herbal beverages and elixirs, and preserve their flavors for year-round enjoyment.

## *Infusing Culinary Dishes*

Cooking is as much an art as it is a science. One of the joys of this culinary journey is experimenting with flavors, and herbs play a central role in this adventure. Infusing culinary dishes with herbs not only elevates the taste but can also provide various health benefits. Here are ways you can use herbs in your dishes:

- **Raw Herbs:** You can chop fresh herbs and sprinkle them over salads, pizzas, or sandwiches. For instance, fresh basil or mint can instantly lift a dish's vibrant aroma and flavor.
- **Cooked into Meals:** Incorporate herbs like rosemary, thyme, or oregano into your cooking process. These can be added to stews, soups, or sauces to impart a deeper flavor profile.
- **Herb-Infused Oils:** Drizzling herb-infused oils over dishes can boost flavor. For example, garlic and rosemary-infused olive oil can be a delightful addition to roasted vegetables.
- **Marinades and Dressings:** Infusing herbs into marinades and dressings can elevate the flavor of meats and salads. Imagine a lemon-thyme marinade for your chicken or a basil vinaigrette for your greens.
- **Stir-fries and Sautés:** Quick-cooking methods like stir-frying or sautéing are great for preserving the fresh flavor of herbs. Toss in some chopped cilantro or basil right at the end to refresh a vegetable stir-fry or a noodle dish.

**Tips:**

- Always wash and pat dry your herbs before cooking to ensure they are free from dirt or pesticides.
- For those new to using herbs, start with a small amount and adjust according to your taste preference.
- Experiment with herb combinations. Some herbs, like basil, oregano, rosemary, and thyme, pair beautifully, enhancing each other's flavors.

## Recipes Incorporating Herbs

To further inspire your herbal culinary journey, here are some simple yet delightful recipes infused with herbs' aromatic flavors. These beginner-friendly recipes will surely be a hit at your next meal.

## Basil and Tomato Bruschetta

A timeless Italian appetizer, this dish combines the vibrant flavors of fresh tomatoes and basil atop crispy toasted baguette slices. The mingling of garlic and extra-virgin olive oil adds a rich depth, while an optional sprinkle of parmesan elevates the experience. A perfect start to any Mediterranean meal.

**Ingredients:**

- 1 baguette, sliced
- 2 cups cherry tomatoes, halved
- 1 cup fresh basil leaves, chopped
- 2 garlic cloves, minced
- 1/4 cup extra-virgin olive oil
- Salt and pepper to taste
- Grated parmesan cheese *(optional)*

**Instructions:**

1. Mix the tomatoes, half of the basil, garlic, salt, and pepper in a bowl.
2. Drizzle olive oil over the baguette slices and toast them until golden brown.
3. Spoon the tomato mixture onto each slice.
4. Garnish with the remaining basil and optional parmesan cheese.

## Rosemary Lemon Grilled Chicken

Venture into a culinary delight with this succulent grilled chicken marinated in a zesty combination of lemon and rosemary. The aromatic garlic and olive oil infuse the meat with a moist and flavorful touch. Whether a summer barbecue or a cozy dinner, this dish promises to be a crowd-pleaser.

**Ingredients:**

- 4 chicken breasts
- 2 lemons, zested and juiced
- 3 rosemary sprigs, finely chopped
- 3 garlic cloves, minced
- 1/4 cup olive oil
- Salt and pepper to taste

**Instructions:**

1. Combine lemon zest, lemon juice, rosemary, garlic, olive oil, salt, and pepper in a bowl. Mix well.
2. Marinate the chicken breasts in the mixture for at least 2 hours.
3. Grill the chicken on medium heat until fully cooked, occasionally basting with the marinade.

## Herb-Crusted Salmon Fillet

Indulge in the rich flavors of the sea paired with a fragrant medley of herbs. This oven-baked salmon fillet boasts a crispy, aromatic crust, blending fresh dill, parsley, and chives with a hint of zesty lemon. Perfectly complemented by a golden breadcrumb finish, it is a delightful dish that promises to impress at any dinner table.

**Ingredients:**

- 2 salmon fillets
- 2 tbsp fresh dill, finely chopped
- 2 tbsp fresh parsley, finely chopped
- 2 tbsp fresh chives, finely chopped
- 1 garlic clove, minced
- Zest of 1 lemon
- 1/4 cup breadcrumbs
- 2 tbsp olive oil
- Salt and pepper to taste

**Instructions:**

1. Preheat oven to 375°F (190°C).
2. Mix the dill, parsley, chives, garlic, lemon zest, breadcrumbs, salt, and pepper in a bowl.
3. Drizzle olive oil over the salmon fillets.
4. Press the herb mixture onto the top of each salmon fillet.
5. Bake in the oven for 15 to 20 minutes or until salmon flakes easily with a fork.

## *Herbal Beverages and Elixirs*

Beyond food, herbs have also found their way into beverages, offering a delightful combination of flavor and therapeutic properties. Herbal beverages and elixirs can be refreshing and healing, providing a natural remedy for various ailments.

### Popular Herbal Beverages

Herbs have long been cherished not just for their culinary prowess but also for their therapeutic properties. From the soothing embrace of warm herbal tea to the refreshing zing of herb-infused waters, the world of herbal beverages offers rich flavors and health benefits. Whether you seek the comfort of traditional decoctions and infusions, the vigor of herb-loaded smoothies, or the sophistication of herbaceous alcoholic concoctions, there is a drink to tantalize every palate.

Here are some popular types:

- **Herbal Teas:** These are a great way to enjoy the essence of herbs. Chamomile can calm your nerves, peppermint can aid digestion, and green tea, with its antioxidants, offers numerous health benefits.
- **Infused Water:** Add a sprig of mint or a slice of cucumber to your water for a refreshing twist. Lemon balm or lavender can also be used to create calming drink infusions.
- **Elixirs:** Typically concentrated liquids that combine herbs with other ingredients like honey or vinegar. Elderberry elixir, for instance, is known for its immune-boosting properties.
- **Decoctions and Infusions:** While many are familiar with the basic concept of herbal teas, there is more depth to herbal drink preparation. Decoctions involve simmering tougher herb parts *(like roots or bark)* to extract their benefits, while infusions involve steeping the more delicate parts *(like leaves or flowers)* in hot water.
- **Smoothies and Juices:** Blending herbs into smoothies and juices is a tasty option for a nutritious start to the day or a midday boost. Consider adding parsley for detoxification, basil for its anti-inflammatory properties, or even cilantro, which can help remove heavy metals from the body.
- **Alcoholic Beverages:** Herbs can also find their way into cocktails and mocktails. An example is the mojito, which uses mint. Or consider infusing spirits with herbs like rosemary for a unique homemade liqueur.

## Recipes for Herbal Beverages and Elixirs

Here are some easy-to-follow recipes to give you a practical glimpse into the world of herbal beverages. They are designed to quench your thirst and provide therapeutic benefits.

## Minty Cucumber Cooler

Refresh and rejuvenate with this invigorating beverage, a harmonious blend of crisp cucumber and fragrant mint. Sweetened with a touch of honey or agave nectar and brought to life with sparkling water, this cooler is both revitalizing and soothing. Garnished with a slice of lemon, it is ideal for a warm day or a palate cleanser between courses.

**Ingredients:**

- 1 cucumber, peeled and chopped
- 10 fresh mint leaves
- 2 tablespoons honey or agave nectar
- Sparkling water
- Ice cubes
- Lemon slices for garnish

**Instructions:**

1. In a blender, combine cucumber, mint leaves, and honey. Blend until smooth.
2. Pour the mixture through a strainer into glasses filled with ice.
3. Top off with sparkling water and garnish with a slice of lemon.

## Ginger-Turmeric Tea

Embark on a journey of warmth and wellness with this aromatic brew. The harmonious blend of ginger and turmeric promises a symphony of flavors and a wealth of health benefits. Renowned for their anti-inflammatory properties, these two potent roots come together in a tea that soothes, revitalizes, and heals. Honey offers a gentle sweetness, while a slice of lemon complements with a zesty finish.

**Ingredients:**

- 1-inch piece of ginger, thinly sliced
- 1-inch piece of turmeric, thinly sliced, or 1 tsp of turmeric powder
- 2 cups of water
- Honey to taste
- Lemon slice for garnish

**Instructions:**

1. In a pot, bring water to a boil.
2. Add ginger and turmeric slices.
3. Simmer for 10 to 15 minutes.
4. Strain into a cup, add honey to taste and garnish with a slice of lemon.

## Lavender Lemonade

Sip on serenity with this delightful twist on a classic drink. The fragrant notes of lavender buds meld beautifully with the tangy freshness of lemon, crafting a refreshing and calming beverage. Whether you are looking to unwind after a long day or seeking a unique thirst quencher for a sunny afternoon, this lemonade, kissed with the essence of lavender, is pure magic in a glass.

**Ingredients:**

- 1/4 cup dried lavender buds
- 2 cups boiling water
- 1 cup fresh lemon juice
- 4 cups cold water
- Honey or agave nectar to taste

**Instructions:**

1. Pour boiling water over lavender buds and steep for 10 minutes.
2. Strain out the lavender and pour the infusion into a pitcher.
3. Add lemon juice, cold water, and sweetener to taste. Stir well.
4. Serve chilled with lemon slices.

## Immunity-Boosting Elixir

Fortify your defenses with this potent concoction that is as flavorful as beneficial. Elderberries, revered for their immune-boosting properties, take center stage, harmonizing with the spicy warmth of ginger and the aromatic allure of cinnamon. Every sip delivers a protective boost, making it a perfect daily tonic for promoting health and warding off ailments.

**Ingredients:**

- 1 cup elderberries
- 4 cups of water
- 1 cinnamon stick
- 1-inch piece of ginger, chopped
- Honey to taste

**Instructions:**

1. In a pot, combine elderberries, water, cinnamon, and ginger.
2. Bring to a boil, then reduce to a simmer for about 45 minutes until the liquid reduces by half.
3. Strain out the solids and let the liquid cool.
4. Add honey to taste and store in a glass bottle in the refrigerator.

## *Incorporating Herbs into Baking*

Baking is one of those delightful culinary arts that comforts and tantalizes the senses. *But have you considered elevating your baked goods by adding a touch of herbal magic?* Imagine the surprise and delight of biting into a familiar treat only to discover a hint of unexpected, aromatic herbal notes that elevate the experience to a new level.

### Herbs in Sweet Bakes

While many people are familiar with herbs in savory dishes, they can be a revelation in sweet bakes. Picture cookies infused with the calming aroma of lavender, a lemon cake subtly laced with rosemary that enhances its citrusy charm, or brownies with a refreshing hint of mint. The combinations might sound unusual at first, but they offer a sophisticated palate experience that is both surprising and delightful.

### Herbs in Savory Bakes

The realm of savory baking offers a plethora of opportunities to incorporate herbs. Imagine biting into a warm scone infused with thyme or focaccia bread, where every bite reveals the flavors of rosemary or basil. Biscuits sprinkled with chives or a tart filled with parsley and cheese can also be a mouth-watering treat.

## Baking Recipes with a Herbal Touch

Delve into herbal baking with a few recipes that beautifully incorporate herbs, turning ordinary baked goods into extraordinary delights.

## Lavender Shortbread Cookies

Indulge in the delicate embrace of these exquisite shortbread cookies, where the timeless charm of buttery goodness meets the ethereal beauty of lavender. With every bite, experience a melt-in-your-mouth sensation with the subtle floral notes of dried lavender buds. Perfect for tea time, these cookies offer an elegant touch to any gathering or a serene moment of solace with your favorite brew.

**Ingredients:**

- 2 cups all-purpose flour
- 1/4 cup sugar
- 1/4 cup powdered sugar
- 1 tbsp dried lavender buds
- 1 cup unsalted butter, softened
- Pinch of salt

**Instructions:**

1. Preheat the oven to 325°F (165°C).
2. Mix flour, sugar, powdered sugar, lavender, and salt in a bowl.
3. Blend in butter until the mixture forms a dough.
4. Roll and cut into desired shapes, then place on a baking sheet.
5. Bake for 15 to 20 minutes until lightly golden. Let cool on a wire rack.

## Rosemary and Olive Oil Bread

Venture into the rustic allure of homemade bread, where the aromatic whispers of rosemary dance with the rich notes of olive oil. This bread, imbued with the fragrant essence of fresh rosemary, promises a hearty and aromatic taste. Whether paired with a soup, adorned with your favorite spread, or savored just as it is, this bread is a testament to the simple pleasures of life and the wonders of baking.

**Ingredients:**

- 3 cups bread flour
- 1 packet of active dry yeast
- 1 tsp sugar
- 1 cup warm water
- 2 tbsp olive oil
- 2 tbsp fresh rosemary, finely chopped
- 1 tsp salt

**Instructions:**

1. Mix the sugar and warm water, then sprinkle the yeast over it. Let sit for 10 minutes until frothy.
2. In a large bowl, combine flour, rosemary, and salt. Pour in the yeast mixture and olive oil.
3. Knead until the dough is smooth and elastic.
4. Place in a greased bowl, cover, and let rise for 1 hour.
5. Preheat the oven to 375°F (190°C).
6. Shape the dough into a loaf and place on a baking sheet.
7. Bake for 20 to 25 minutes until golden brown.

## Herbal Wellness Routines

Throughout history, cultures around the world have tapped into the wisdom of plants, integrating them into daily rituals that promote wellness from the inside out. Herbalism wonders that it bridges the past and the present, allowing modern-day individuals to harness the time-tested benefits of plants in their daily lives.

### *Morning and Evening Herbal Rituals*

How one begins and concludes one's day plays a profound role in shaping overall well-being. The rituals we adopt can either energize you for the day ahead or provide the tranquility necessary for rejuvenation at night. Infusing these daily routines with the power of herbs allows for a deeper connection to nature and can significantly enhance mental and physical vitality.

#### Morning Rituals

Mornings are a time of rebirth, where the world awakens from its nocturnal slumber. Infusing this sacred time with herbal practices can set the tone for a day filled with purpose and vitality. Whether it is the antioxidant-rich embrace of green tea or the adaptogenic strengths of ashwagandha, these rituals serve as a bridge, helping you navigate the day's journey with clarity and energy.

**Herbal Teas:**

- **Green Tea Ritual:** Prepare a warm cup of green tea upon waking. As you sip, not only are you ingesting antioxidants, but you are also embracing a moment of mindfulness to start your day.
- **Peppermint Tea Boost:** Opt for peppermint tea if you want a revitalizing kick. Its refreshing aroma can clear morning grogginess, and its digestive properties make it an excellent post-breakfast choice.

**Tinctures and Tonics:**

- **Ashwagandha Morning Elixir:** Begin by sourcing a high-quality ashwagandha tincture. Mix a few drops with a glass of water or juice each morning. Consuming this adaptogenic herb helps fortify the body against daily stressors and can increase vitality.
- **Ginseng Boost:** Ginseng is another adaptogenic herb known for its energy-enhancing properties. Integrate a ginseng tonic into your breakfast routine as a standalone shot or mixed into your morning smoothie.

**Evening Rituals**

As evening approaches and the day winds down, it is essential to transition to a more peaceful mindset. Incorporating herbal rituals, such as calming chamomile tea or a soothing lavender bath, can help relax your body and mind, setting the stage for a good night's sleep.

**Relaxing Teas:**

- **Chamomile Nightcap:** As the evening winds down, brew chamomile tea. Its gentle, apple-like aroma soothes the senses. Sipping on chamomile can aid digestion and prepare the mind for a peaceful night's sleep.
- **Valerian Root Tranquility:** Consider valerian root tea for those particularly restless nights. Its strong, woody taste might be an acquired one, but its benefits as a sleep aid are well-documented.

**Herbal Baths:**

- **Lavender Bath Soak:** As part of your nighttime routine, draw a warm bath and add a few drops of lavender essential oil or a sachet of dried lavender flowers. The aromatic experience works wonders in releasing muscular tension and clearing mental clutter. As you soak, let the day's worries drift away, enveloped by lavender's calming embrace.

- **Eucalyptus Steam Session:** If you feel congested or want a refreshing bath experience, sprinkle a few drops of eucalyptus essential oil into your bath or shower. The steam combined with eucalyptus can open the airways and provide a refreshing end to the day.

## Boosting Mood and Well-being with Aromatics

Aromas have an uncanny ability to evoke memories, alter moods, and influence overall well-being. Aromatic herbs, packed with fragrant essences, harness this power to offer a natural way to elevate mood and promote wellness. Incorporating them into daily routines can set the tone for your day, shift your mood, and tap into the deep-rooted connection between scent and emotion.

### *Uplifting Scents*

As the pace of daily life quickens, moments of invigoration can be vital. Turning to nature, specific scents can enliven the senses, gifting you with a burst of energy and clarity.

- **Rosemary Boost:** A whiff of rosemary, either through essential oil or a freshly crushed sprig, can invigorate the mind and enhance memory. It is a perfect companion for those mid-morning slumps or when you need to sharpen your focus.
- **Basil Delight:** The crisp scent of basil can uplift your mood and bring a sense of alertness. Consider growing a basil plant on your desk or workspace and taking moments throughout the day to rub its leaves and inhale its rejuvenating aroma.

### Daily Activities

Start your morning with a rosemary-infused shower. Simply hang fresh rosemary sprigs under the showerhead, allowing the steam to release its energizing aroma. Craft a personal aromatic spray in a spray bottle by combining a few drops of basil essential oil with water. Use it to refresh your space throughout the day.

## *Calming Aromatics*

In a world where constant stimulation is the norm, the value of tranquility cannot be overstated. Certain aromas act as portals to serenity, helping you navigate the turbulent tides of life.

- **Lavender's Embrace:** Known for its relaxing properties, lavender's gentle scent can prepare you for restful sleep or help you decompress after a hectic day.
- **Chamomile's Tranquility:** While often consumed as tea, the aroma of chamomile also has soothing effects, making it ideal for moments when you seek calm.

### Daily Activities

Before bedtime, sprinkle a few drops of lavender essential oil onto your pillow to encourage restful sleep. Lighting a chamomile-scented candle creates a calming ambiance in your evening relaxation zone.

## *Tips for Using Aromatics and Scents:*

- Essential oils are potent. Always dilute them using carrier oil *(almond or coconut oil)* for topical applications and ensure they are dispersed properly when diffusing.
- Explore making sachets filled with dried aromatic herbs. Place these in drawers, closets, or even your car to subtly introduce these scents into your daily life.

- For those sensitive to strong scents, consider opting for hydrosols, gentler aromatic waters derived from distilling plant materials.

## Herbal Gardens and Landscaping

The idea of cultivating a personal space filled with greenery and natural remedies offers a rejuvenating escape amidst the constant hustle and bustle of the city. Herbal gardens, especially those set up indoors, are not just a source of fresh flavors for your culinary adventures but also serve as sanctuaries of health and aesthetic pleasure. As city dwellers increasingly grapple with space constraints, the allure of an indoor garden—a personal Eden amid urban chaos—grows ever stronger.

### *Starting Your Herbal Garden*

The appeal of home-grown herbs is not just in their freshness or the fact that they are free of pesticides. It is also about the sense of accomplishment in nurturing something from seed to plant and the joy of having nature's bounty within the confines of your home.

#### Picking the Right Location

Location is paramount for plants. While focusing on indoor settings, you can consider these locations for indoor gardening:

- **Window Sills:** Ideal for smaller pots, these naturally sunlit platforms can house several herbs. A south or west-facing window sill ensures the herbs get sunlight for growth.
- **Balconies and Patios:** If you have a balcony or a small patio, it can be an extended indoor space, especially for larger plants or for experimenting with mini herb trees.

- **Indoor Green Shelves:** For homes lacking window spaces, shelves equipped with LED grow lights can simulate sunlight, ensuring herbs get their required light dosage.

## Choosing the Herbs

Herb selection can be based on multiple factors, such as your culinary preferences, therapeutic needs, or simply the herbs' aesthetic appeal.

- **Culinary Staples:** Basil, for its sweet aroma, is a kitchen favorite. Rosemary, with its pine-like flavor, can elevate dishes. Chives, with a hint of garlic, are great garnishes.
- **Medicinal Mavens:** Consider planting aloe vera or echinacea for its skin-soothing properties, which are known to boost immunity.
- **Aesthetic Appeal:** Some herbs are grown simply for their beauty. Lavender, with its purple hue and calming scent, or the silver-green sage, can be a visual delight.

## Soil and Containers

The right environment at the roots ensures the herbs grow healthy and happy. Take note of the following:

- **Soil Mix:** A lightweight, well-draining potting mix is essential. Some gardeners also recommend adding a bit of sand or perlite to enhance drainage.
- **Containers:** The market today offers a plethora of options. Traditional terracotta pots are breathable, ensuring the roots get ample air. Plastic pots are lightweight and retain moisture longer. Whichever you choose, ensure it has drainage holes. Overwatering is a common mistake in indoor gardening; these holes prevent water from stagnating.

- **Personal Touch:** Personalizing pots can also be a fun activity. Paint them, stick labels, or even carve out names. This adds a decorative touch and can be a fun weekend DIY project.

## *Maintaining and Harvesting Herbs*

As you watch your herbs grow, their needs evolve, too. To ensure your herbal plants not only survive but thrive, it is important to understand the intricacies of their care. Regular care, affection, and timely maintenance can lead to flourishing indoor herb gardens. It is a relationship – the more love and understanding you show your plants, the more they reward you with aromatic foliage and a sense of accomplishment. These everyday practices can make or break the health of your herbal oasis.

### Watering Your Plants

Just as each herb has its unique flavor and aroma, their watering needs can also differ. Here are some tips.

- **Feel the Soil:** Before reaching for that watering can, stick your finger into the soil up to an inch deep. If it feels dry, it is time to water.
- **Watering Technique:** It is best to water the base of the plant to prevent fungal issues on the leaves. For pots without saucers, ensure excess water can escape to avoid root rot.
- **Mind the Humidity:** Some herbs, like basil, thrive in higher humidity. Consider using a tray filled with water and pebbles near your plants in drier conditions or colder months to increase ambient moisture.

## Pruning and Encouraging Growth

Trimming your herbs is not just about harvesting; it is a growth encouragement tactic. To help you with this, follow these:

- **Strategic Snipping:** Focus on the top growth, encouraging the plant to branch out. Over time, this can lead to a fuller, bushier appearance.
- **Avoiding Flowering:** If you notice your herbs starting to flower, pinch those buds off. While flowers are pretty, they can lead to a bitter taste in many herbs.
- **Rotation Routine:** Indoor plants tend to grow towards their light source. Rotating them every few days ensures even growth.

## Harvesting Tips

The following are harvesting tips:

- **Timing Matters:** Early morning, when the plant's essential oils are most concentrated, is the best time for harvesting.
- **Clean Cuts:** Using a sharp, clean pair of scissors or pruners reduces stress on the plant and prevents potential damage.
- **Mindful Harvesting:** While the temptation might be to harvest a lot, always allow your plant enough leaves to continue with photosynthesis. This ensures sustained growth and repeated harvests.

## *Indoor Herbal Planters*

Bringing nature indoors has multiple benefits – from purifying air to elevating moods. When this greenery is also a source of natural remedies, it is doubly beneficial. Explore the innovative ways to incorporate herbal planters indoors and discuss some key medicinal herbs to consider.

### Vertical Planters

Maximizing space while ensuring your herbs get adequate sunlight is the goal. Some examples are:

- **Hanging Pockets:** Made of felt or fabric, these planters can be suspended on walls and filled with various herbs.
- **Ladder Planters:** An old wooden ladder can be repurposed to accommodate multiple pots, creating a rustic herbal corner.

### Mason Jar Planters

Eco-friendly and chic, mason jars can be turned into mini herb havens. Remember, though, they lack drainage holes, so a layer of charcoal or pebbles at the base can prevent root rot.

### Tiered Stands

Place these in a sunny corner or by a window, and you have a rotating carousel of your favorite herbs.

### Recycled Containers

The sky's the limit here. Old boots, ceramic bowls, or tin cans can be refurbished into quirky planters. Ensure you drill holes for drainage, and they are good to go.

### Medicinal Herbs for Indoor Planting

Beyond the culinary realm, some herbs serve as natural medicine cabinets. Growing them indoors means you have remedies right when you need them.

- **Aloe Vera:** This succulent is not just ornamental. Its gel can soothe burns, moisturize skin, and aid digestion.

- **Lavender:** Beyond its delightful aroma, lavender is known for its calming properties. A pot of lavender in your bedroom can aid relaxation and sleep.
- **Peppermint:** This herb's invigorating scent can relieve headaches and improve focus. Additionally, peppermint tea aids digestion.
- **Lemon Balm:** A close relative of mint, lemon balm is known for its calming effects, making it beneficial for those with anxiety or sleep disturbances.
- **Chamomile:** These dainty flowers are more than decorative. Brewing them into tea can help with sleep and alleviate digestive discomfort.

## Exercise: A Day of Herbal Living

This activity will help you integrate herbalism into a single day by providing a hands-on experience incorporating herbs into daily life, from meals and beverages to wellness routines.

**Materials:**

- Various fresh or dried herbs *(basil, rosemary, mint, chamomile, lavender, etc.)*
- Cooking ingredients for your chosen meals
- Teapot or infuser for herbal beverages
- Essential oils or dried herbs for aromatics *(optional)*
- Notebook or journal for reflection
- Small pot or planter *(for indoor herbal planter activity)*

**Instructions:**

1. **Morning Herbal Ritual:** Begin your day with a refreshing herbal tea. Consider a combination of mint and chamomile or rosemary and lemon balm. As you sip, focus on the flavors and how they make you feel. Use a spritz of

rose water or a few drops of lavender essential oil on your wrists to help you feel refreshed and awake.

2. **Cooking with Herbs for Breakfast:** Incorporate herbs into your breakfast. Ideas could be adding basil to your omelet, sprinkling dried oregano on your avocado toast, or blending fresh mint into your morning smoothie. As you eat, take notes on how the herbs enhance or change the flavor of your dish.
3. **Mid-Day Herbal Beverage:** Prepare a cold herbal elixir. Consider making rosemary lemonade or mint-infused water.
4. **Lunch Incorporating Herbal Flavors:** Make a simple salad with fresh or dried herbs. You could also prepare an herbal dressing using basil, garlic, olive oil, and lemon juice. As you enjoy your lunch, reflect on how the herbs contribute to the taste and texture of your meal.
5. **Afternoon Aromatics Boost:** Boost your mood with aromatics. Use an essential oil diffuser with oils like lavender or eucalyptus, or simply place dried aromatic herbs in a bowl on your desk.
6. **Herbal Garden Exploration:** Spend time in your or nearby herbal garden. If you cannot access one, consider starting your indoor herbal planter now. Plant an herb like basil, parsley, or chives. Journal about your experience, the scents, the touch of the leaves, and the ambiance of the garden space.
7. **Evening Herbal Rituals:** Wind down with an evening herbal tea like chamomile or valerian root. Consider taking a bath with lavender or rose petals for relaxation. Before bed, reflect on your day in your journal. Write down how the various herbal interventions and any favorites you discovered made you feel.
8. **Reflection:** At the end of the day, review your journal. Reflect on how herbalism enhanced your day, which practices you might want to incorporate regularly, and any discoveries or inspirations.

# CHAPTER 7

# Advanced Herbal Applications

Now, you will explore how herbs can manage chronic issues like pain and inflammation and support critical aspects of health like heart function and blood sugar regulation. Detoxification is also covered, focusing on daily herbal cleansing rituals and more intensive detox diets.

The chapter highlights key herbs, their traditional uses, and scientific backing. You will discover time-tested botanical remedies ranging from turmeric to milk thistle and how these can be incorporated into your lifestyle. Lifestyle factors like diet, exercise, and stress reduction are also discussed as part of a holistic approach.

## Managing Chronic Pain and Inflammation

Chronic pain and inflammation stand out prominently among the different ailments that many experience. *But what can one do to manage such discomfort?* This section addresses this pressing question by exploring conventional pain medications, joint and muscle pain peculiarities, and lifestyle changes that can complement herbal treatments.

## *Pain Medications*

Pain medications have been a go-to solution for those experiencing chronic pain. However, it is essential to understand their mechanisms, benefits, and potential side effects. Let us delve into the intricacies of these drugs, how they function, and possible herbal alternatives for them.

### How Pain Medication Works

Pain medications, commonly known as analgesics, block pain signals from reaching the brain or alter the brain's interpretation of those signals. There are two primary categories: over-the-counter (OTC) drugs, such as ibuprofen or acetaminophen, and prescription medications like opioids.

OTC pain relievers provide quick relief from minor aches and pains for many. Prescription pain medications, especially opioids, can be effective for more severe pain but come with caution.

While OTC drugs might seem harmless, prolonged usage can lead to issues like stomach ulcers or liver damage. On the other hand, opioids have a high risk of addiction and can cause respiratory depression.

### Herbal Alternatives to Pain Medications

As individuals become more aware of potential side effects from standard pain medications, many are turning to herbal alternatives for relief. These plant-based remedies have been used for centuries across various cultures, offering a more natural approach to pain management. This section will explore some popular herbal alternatives and their potential benefits.

- **Willow Bark:** Historically, people have chewed the bark of the willow tree to relieve pain and inflammation. The active ingredient, salicin, is similar to modern-day aspirin. Today, willow bark can be consumed as tea or as a supplement.
- **Devil's Claw:** Originating from South Africa, the devil's claw has roots that can relieve pain, particularly in the back and joints. Studies suggest it might benefit osteoarthritis and rheumatoid arthritis due to its anti-inflammatory properties.
- **Arnica:** This herb, often found in mountainous regions, is commonly used for bruises, swelling, and pain relief. It can be applied topically as a gel or cream. However, it should not be applied to broken skin or open wounds.
- **Ginger:** Not just a kitchen spice, ginger has potent anti-inflammatory properties. Consuming ginger tea or supplements can benefit individuals with osteoarthritis or rheumatoid arthritis. A study even found that ginger extract reduced osteoarthritic pain when applied topically.
- **Turmeric:** Closely related to ginger, turmeric contains the active ingredient curcumin, which possesses strong anti-inflammatory properties. It can help reduce pain and discomfort from various conditions, including joint pains.

## *Joint and Muscle Pain*

Many people experience joint and muscle pain due to arthritis or muscle strain. Understanding the nature of this pain and its causes can guide appropriate management strategies.

### Causes

Joint pain often arises from joint inflammation, commonly seen in arthritis. Muscle pain, on the other hand, may result from overuse, strain, or direct injury. Sometimes, diseases like fibromyalgia or infections can also cause muscle pain.

## Benefits of Using Natural Remedies for Joint and Muscle Pain

Natural remedies have long been the cornerstone of many traditional healing practices. Their usage for joint and muscle pain, in particular, has grown in popularity due to several benefits over conventional medications. Here is why many choose the herbal path for pain management.

### Fewer Side Effects

One of the most touted advantages of herbal remedies is reduced side effects. Unlike many over-the-counter or prescription pain medications, which can cause stomach issues, liver damage, or addiction, herbal remedies tend to have milder side effects when used appropriately.

### Holistic Healing

Herbal remedies often do not just address the symptom (pain) but aim to treat the root cause, like inflammation. For example, turmeric alleviates pain and reduces inflammation in the body, leading to more comprehensive healing.

### Cost-Effective

Over time, relying on prescription medications can become expensive, even with insurance. In contrast, many herbal remedies, like ginger or willow bark, are more affordable and accessible.

### Sustainability

Natural remedies, especially those grown locally, have a lesser environmental footprint. No industrial production is involved, making it a more sustainable choice for those who are environmentally conscious.

### Versatility

Many herbal remedies have multiple uses. For instance, ginger, while beneficial for joint pain, also aids in digestion and can boost the immune system. This multifunctionality means you are addressing one issue and potentially improving various aspects of your health.

### Empowerment

Taking control of one's health through natural means can be empowering. By understanding the herbs and their effects, individuals can make informed choices, fostering a sense of autonomy over their well-being.

### Herbal Remedies

Several herbs have been traditionally used to address joint and muscle pain. For instance, turmeric and its active component, curcumin, have anti-inflammatory properties, making them useful for joint pain. Capsaicin, found in chili peppers, can be used topically to relieve muscle pain by reducing pain signals.

## *Lifestyle Changes to Complement Herbal Therapies*

Incorporating herbal remedies can be beneficial, but for holistic healing and pain management, certain lifestyle changes can complement these natural treatments. By adopting specific lifestyle changes and pairing them with herbal therapies, you can create a comprehensive approach to managing chronic pain and inflammation. Remember, it is essential to tailor these strategies to your unique needs and circumstances, and always consult with healthcare professionals when making significant changes to your regimen.

Here is how you can enhance your pain relief journey.

- **Exercise:** Regular movement can help ease pain, especially for those with arthritis. Activities like walking, swimming, or yoga can increase flexibility and strength without putting too much strain on the body.
- **Diet:** Eating an anti-inflammatory diet filled with fruits, vegetables, whole grains, and lean proteins can reduce inflammation. Foods rich in omega-3 fatty acids, such as fish or flaxseeds, can also help.
- **Stress Management:** Chronic pain and stress often go hand in hand. Mindfulness practices like meditation, deep breathing, or even hobbies can reduce stress and, in turn, pain.
- **Sleep:** Getting adequate rest is crucial. When sleep-deprived, the body might produce inflammatory cytokines, exacerbating pain.
- **Hydration:** Water plays a vital role in the health of our joints and muscles. Keeping hydrated helps maintain the lubrication of the joints, aiding in reducing pain and stiffness. Besides, water helps flush out toxins from the body, which might contribute to inflammation. Aim for at least 8 glasses daily, and increase intake if you're active or in a hot environment.
- **Posture and Ergonomics:** How you sit, stand, and move can greatly influence the stress on your joints and muscles. Proper posture reduces strain and can prevent or alleviate pain. If you work at a desk, ensure your workstation is ergonomically set up to minimize strain. Also, consider tools like standing desks or ergonomic chairs.
- **Weight Management:** Excess weight puts additional pressure on joints, particularly on weight-bearing ones like the knees and hips. Losing weight, even a small amount, can significantly reduce joint pain. Combining a balanced diet with regular exercise, as mentioned above, can aid in effective weight management.

- **Heat and Cold Therapy:** Simple yet effective, warm compresses can help relax and loosen tissues and stimulate blood flow to the area. On the other hand, cold compresses can reduce inflammation and numb the area, thereby alleviating pain. Depending on the nature of your pain, alternating between the two might be beneficial.
- **Limit Alcohol and Tobacco:** Both alcohol and tobacco can interfere with the effectiveness of some medications and can exacerbate the conditions causing pain. Cutting down or quitting can improve your overall health and, in turn, reduce chronic pain.
- **Massage:** Therapeutic massage can benefit many types of pain, especially muscle pain. It helps increase circulation, relaxes muscles, and releases stored tension. Consider visiting a certified massage therapist who can tailor the session to your needs.

## Herbs for Heart Health and Diabetes

With the rising number of people facing heart issues and diabetes around the world, there is a growing interest in finding natural ways to help manage these conditions. Many look to herbs, which have been used for thousands of years to treat various ailments. Some herbs, like hawthorn, support heart health, while others, like cinnamon, can help regulate blood sugar. This section will explore these herbs and learn how they can play a role in heart health and diabetes care, bridging ancient wisdom with modern understanding.

### *Blood Pressure Management*

Blood pressure is more than just numbers on a monitor; it indicates cardiovascular health. High blood pressure, or hypertension, can silently damage the heart over time, leading to severe complications if left unchecked. While conventional medications play an essential role in management, herbal remedies have shown promise in offering unique benefits without many side effects linked to pharmaceuticals. Here is a deeper look into herbal solutions for blood pressure management.

### *The Herbal Advantage*

One of the standout reasons people turn to herbal remedies for blood pressure management is their multifaceted approach. Unlike single-action drugs, herbs often contain many active compounds that work in harmony, targeting various aspects of the issue. Additionally, many herbs help manage blood pressure and offer other cardiovascular benefits like improving heart muscle function or reducing arterial plaque.

## Herbs to Use

Here are the common herbs to use for blood pressure management.

- **Hawthorn:** A venerable tree with a long history in traditional medicine, the hawthorn plant stands out in cardiovascular care. Hawthorn's magic lies in its array of flavonoids, which are believed to enhance the heart's pumping action, improve blood flow, and even reduce symptoms of heart failure. When it comes to blood pressure, hawthorn helps relax and open up blood vessels, facilitating better circulation and potentially easing hypertension.
- **Garlic:** Beyond its robust aroma and flavor, garlic has potent medicinal qualities. Its primary active component, allicin, releases hydrogen sulfide when ingested. This gas helps relax blood vessels and enhance blood flow. Moreover, garlic has a diuretic effect, promoting the elimination of excess sodium and water from the body, further aiding in blood pressure reduction.

- **Celery Seed:** While less common than garlic and hawthorn, celery seed is a gem in herbal blood pressure remedies. Traditional Chinese medicine has utilized celery seeds to promote relaxation and lower blood pressure. Phthalides, active compounds in celery seeds, can help relax artery walls and reduce inflammation, both crucial for maintaining healthy blood pressure levels.

## *Cholesterol Balance*

Cholesterol plays a dual role in the body. While it is a fundamental building block for cell membranes and is used to make hormones and vitamin D, an imbalance, particularly an excess of bad cholesterol, can be detrimental. High cholesterol levels increase the risk of atherosclerosis, a condition where plaque builds up inside the arteries. Over time, this buildup can narrow the arteries, limit blood flow, and raise the risk of heart attacks and strokes. Therefore, striking a balance in cholesterol levels becomes paramount for heart health and overall well-being.

### The Importance of Cholesterol Balance

Balancing cholesterol is vital for several reasons:

- **Reduced Risk of Cardiovascular Diseases:** High LDL cholesterol levels in the blood can lead to plaque buildup in arteries, increasing the chances of heart attacks and strokes.
- **Improved Blood Flow:** Balanced cholesterol ensures that blood can flow freely through the arteries, efficiently delivering oxygen and nutrients to various body parts.
- **Overall Cell Health:** While high cholesterol is harmful, the body still requires cholesterol for cellular functions. Striking a balance ensures cells function optimally without the risk of arterial clogs.

### Herbs to Use

Nature has provided herbs that can aid in maintaining cholesterol balance. Here are some examples:

- **Fenugreek:** A staple in many Asian dishes, fenugreek seeds are not just culinary marvels. They contain saponins that can bind to cholesterol molecules, preventing their absorption in the intestines and aiding their excretion, helping lower LDL cholesterol levels.
- **Red Yeast Rice:** A product of rice fermented with the yeast Monascus purpureus, red yeast rice has been used in traditional Chinese medicine for centuries. Its cholesterol-lowering effects are attributed to monacolin K, which inhibits an enzyme involved in cholesterol synthesis in the liver.
- **Artichoke Leaf Extract:** This extract, derived from the leaves of the artichoke plant, can boost bile production in the liver, helping to excrete more cholesterol. Additionally, its antioxidant properties may protect LDL cholesterol from oxidation, a process known to exacerbate arterial plaque buildup.

## *Blood Sugar Regulation*

Blood sugar regulation is at the heart of metabolic health. Imbalances, whether high or low, can lead to a slew of complications ranging from fatigue and blurred vision to more severe outcomes like nerve damage or cardiovascular disease. Notably, while several herbs have been identified for their potential to lower blood sugar, some herbs can raise sugar levels, underscoring the importance of reasonable use.

## The Dual Role of Herbs

Herbs, in their natural complexity, can serve multiple functions. Some can lower blood sugar, making them useful for those with diabetes or high blood sugar. Others, however, can elevate sugar levels. This property might be beneficial for individuals with hypoglycemia *(low blood sugar)* but can be detrimental for others. This dual role underlines the importance of understanding individual health needs and consulting a healthcare provider before introducing any herbal regimen.

## Herbs to Use

In this section, you will explore herbs influencing blood sugar, lowering and raising this.

- **Cinnamon:** This aromatic spice, often associated with sweet treats, has an unexpected role in blood sugar regulation. Cinnamon can enhance insulin sensitivity, ensuring the body uses this hormone more effectively, ultimately lowering blood sugar levels.
- **Berberine:** Extracted from plants like barberry, goldenseal, and Oregon grape, berberine is a compound with a golden track record in traditional medicine. It operates by activating an enzyme called AMPK, which improves insulin sensitivity, thereby helping reduce blood sugar levels.
- **Bitter Melon:** Its unique appearance aside, bitter melon is known in several cultures for its medicinal properties. It contains compounds that act similarly to insulin, aiding in glucose uptake by cells and thus can help manage blood sugar levels.

### Herbs That Can Raise Blood Sugar

While the focus is often on herbs that lower blood sugar, some herbs can elevate it. For instance, when consumed in large amounts, licorice root can increase blood sugar levels. While this might be useful for those who experience bouts of low blood sugar, it is a concern for others, particularly diabetics.

## Detoxification and Cleansing with Herbs

Detoxification, or removing toxins and unwanted substances from the body, has been practiced for centuries across cultures. While our bodies are naturally equipped with detoxifying systems, certain herbs can support and enhance these processes.

### *Daily Detoxifying Herbs and Teas*

Imagine starting each day with a ritual that not only warms you but also aids in purifying your body. Many herbs and teas can be incorporated into daily routines to support general detoxification, ensuring you are cleansing little by little every day.

- **Milk Thistle Tea:** Milk thistle, known for its active ingredient, silymarin, is often lauded for its liver-protecting qualities. It has been used for centuries to support liver health and to assist in detoxification processes.
- **Burdock Root Tea:** Burdock root is known for its blood-purifying abilities. It helps in eliminating toxins from the bloodstream and improving overall skin health.
- **Dandelion Tea:** Often regarded as a pesky weed, dandelion is a detox powerhouse. Its roots and leaves support the liver, helping it break down fats and produce amino acids.
- **Nettle Tea:** This stinging plant, when brewed as tea, acts as a natural diuretic, aiding the kidneys in filtering and flushing out toxins.

### *Organ-Specific Cleansing (Liver, Kidneys, Lungs)*

While daily detox rituals benefit the entire system, sometimes specific organs require targeted support. This section discusses herbs that can aid the liver, kidneys, and lungs in their detoxification roles.

- **Liver:** Milk thistle, with its active component silymarin, shields the liver from toxins and promotes liver cell growth. Turmeric, with its main compound curcumin, further protects the liver from damage and aids in its regeneration.
- **Kidneys:** Cranberries are not just for urinary tract infections; they prevent bacteria from sticking to the kidneys. Juniper berries stimulate the kidneys and bladder, enhancing their toxin-flushing capabilities.
- **Lungs:** Mullein has been traditionally used to clear excess mucus from the lungs, aiding in respiratory detoxification. Eucalyptus, when inhaled, promotes respiratory health by dilating the blood vessels, allowing more oxygen into the lungs.

### *Herbal Fasting and Detox Diets*

Beyond daily practices and organ-specific herbs, there is an arena of more intensive detoxification methods: herbal fasting and detox diets. These regimens can reset and rejuvenate the body but must be approached with caution.

- **Herbal Fasting:** Incorporating herbs into a fasting regimen can provide nutrients and support to the body when it is not receiving its regular caloric intake. For example, using ginger during a fast can promote digestion and alleviate nausea.
- **Detox Diets:** These are short-term dietary interventions aimed at eliminating toxins. Incorporating herbs like cilan-

tro, which can bind to heavy metals and help remove them, can be beneficial. Another herb, burdock root, purifies the blood, assisting in toxin removal.

## Tips for Herbal Fasting and Detox Diets

While the benefits of herbal fasting and detox diets can be alluring, it is essential to follow specific guidelines to ensure safety and effectiveness. Here are some general pointers to keep in mind:

- **Consult a Healthcare Professional First:** Before starting any detox or fasting regimen, it is paramount to consult with a nutritionist, naturopath, or doctor to ensure it is appropriate for your specific health conditions and needs.
- **Stay Hydrated:** Drink plenty of water. Fasting and detoxification can increase toxin elimination, and staying hydrated will assist in flushing these out and preventing dehydration.
- **Listen to Your Body:** If you feel excessively tired, dizzy, or unwell, it might be a sign that the detox or fast is not right for you. Always prioritize your well-being.

## Herbal Fasting Guidelines

By giving your digestive system a break and introducing beneficial herbs, you can enhance the elimination of toxins and potentially boost overall well-being. Keep these in mind when herbal fasting:

- **Duration:** A typical herbal fast might last anywhere from 24 hours to 3 days for beginners. Extending beyond this without professional guidance can be risky.
- **Herb Selection:** Opt for herbs that support digestion and detoxification, like ginger, peppermint, or dandelion.
- **Preparation:** Begin by reducing your intake of caffeine, sugar, and processed foods a few days before the fast.

- **Breaking the Fast:** Introduce foods slowly, starting with easily digestible foods like broths or smoothies.

## Detox Diet Guidelines

A detox diet emphasizes foods and practices that assist the body in clearing out toxins. Through this dietary approach, the aim is to rejuvenate the body, support liver function, and improve energy levels. Follow the guidelines below for a Detox diet.

- **Duration:** Most detox diets are short-term and might last from 3 days to 2 weeks.
- **Diet Composition:** Focus on whole foods, such as fresh fruits, vegetables, nuts, and seeds. Avoid processed foods, alcohol, caffeine, and sugar.
- **Herb Selection:** Incorporate detoxifying herbs like cilantro, burdock root, milk thistle, and nettle. These can be consumed as teas, tinctures, or in supplement form.
- **Post-Detox Transition:** Once your detox diet is completed, slowly reintroduce other foods to prevent digestive discomfort.

# CHAPTER 8

# The Spiritual Dimension of Herbalism

In this chapter, you are invited to explore the spiritual dimension of herbalism, a journey that reveals the profound connections you can form with plants. Beyond their physical existence, plants possess a spiritual essence capable of nurturing, guiding, and healing on a deeper level. You'll delve into the ancient and symbiotic relationship between humans and plants, discovering how indigenous cultures have long recognized and revered the spiritual energy of plants. This exploration will take you through various aspects of plant spirituality, including the role of plants as spiritual companions, the practice of plant meditation, and the significance of rituals and ceremonies.

This chapter opens doors to understanding how plants can be more than just physical healers; they can also offer spiritual guidance and insight. You'll learn about different spiritual plants and their unique roles in various cultural practices, and you'll be introduced to the fascinating interplay between ethnobotany and sacred plant traditions. Through this journey, you'll gain a deeper appreciation of how plants have been woven into the spiritual fabric of human history and how they continue to offer profound insights and connections in the modern world.

## Plants as Spiritual Companions

The deeper you venture into the realm of natural medicine and herbal remedies, the clearer it becomes that plants are not just physical entities. They possess a spiritual essence that can nurture, guide, and heal on a deeper level. This chapter introduces the spiritual dimension of herbalism, revealing the profound connections that can be formed with plants and how they can be spiritual companions on our life's journey. This section discusses three pivotal aspects of this dimension: Plant Spirit Medicine, Plant Meditation, and Rituals and Ceremonies.

### *Plant Spirit Medicine*

Plant Spirit Medicine delves into the idea that plants are not just physical entities. Beyond their tangible presence, they possess an essence, a spirit that resonates with the rhythms of the universe. This spirit, imbued with consciousness and wisdom, offers a pathway to healing, guidance, and deeper understanding.

#### The Ancient Bond

Throughout human history, the symbiotic relationship between plants and people has been evident. Our ancestors didn't just view plants as food or medicine in the physical sense; they recognized and revered the spiritual energy emanating from them.

For countless generations, indigenous cultures have believed that plants are sentient beings. They communicate, they understand, and they offer guidance. Shamans, the bridge between the spiritual and physical worlds, would often venture into trances aided by plants to gain insights, ask for healing, or seek prophecies. The spirit of the plant wasn't a metaphor but a genuine, conscious entity that interacted with the shaman.

## The Spirituality of Plants

So, how can a plant be spiritual? At the core of this belief is the understanding that everything in the universe carries energy, a life force. Plants, with their roots deeply embedded in the Earth and their leaves reaching out to the sun, act as bridges between the terrestrial and celestial energies. Their growth and lifecycle are in tune with the rhythms of the Earth, the seasons, and cosmic cycles.

Furthermore, plants often thrive in communities. Just as a human community has individuals with different roles and responsibilities, plants in a forest or meadow have roles – from providing shelter to transferring nutrients. This sense of purpose and interconnectedness reflects a deeper consciousness, a spiritual layer that humans can tap into.

### *Examples of Spiritual Plants*

Here are some examples of spiritual plants, some of which are also treated as medicines.

- **Ayahuasca:** The brew made from the Banisteriopsis caapi vine and the leaves of the Psychotria viridis plant is more than just a concoction with psychoactive properties. For the indigenous cultures of the Amazon, Ayahuasca is a sacred medicine allowing them to communicate with the spirits of the forest and their ancestors. The visions and insights experienced under its influence are often transformative, offering healing and clarity.
- **Tobacco Rituals:** In many Native American traditions, tobacco is viewed as a powerful spiritual ally. It's not consumed casually but is used in rituals and offerings. When smoked in a ceremonial pipe, the rising smoke is seen as carrying prayers to the Creator. The act is deeply spiritual, a dialogue between humans, plants, and the divine.

- **The Blue Lotus:** Ancient Egyptians revered the Blue Lotus. They believed the flower to be a representation of the sun and rebirth. Consuming the flower, often in a brewed concoction, was said to lead to a state of bliss and deeper understanding, making it a part of many spiritual rituals.

### *Plant Meditation*

Meditating with plants offers a unique pathway to stillness and insight. Plant Meditation is about connecting with a plant on an energetic level, absorbing its essence, and understanding its wisdom.

When you sit in meditation with a plant, you're not just focusing on its physical form. Instead, you're tuning into its energy, its life force, its spirit. It's an invitation to connect, listen, and understand the plant at a deeper level.

For instance, if you choose to meditate with a rose, you might feel its essence of love, beauty, and compassion seeping into your consciousness. Meditating with sage might bring about feelings of purification and clarity. This practice invites you to form a bond with plants, one where you can listen to their silent whispers and messages.

### *Rituals and Ceremonies*

Rituals and ceremonies are structured practices that allow individuals to honor, celebrate, or seek guidance from the plant spirits. These practices are as varied as the cultures they originate from, yet they all underscore a deep reverence for the plant world.

Rituals are a means of establishing a sacred space, setting intentions, and connecting with the spiritual realm. They often involve specific actions, words, and sometimes even dance and music.

Through these ceremonies, participants can tap into the power of plants, seeking their blessings, guidance, or healing.

**Examples of Plant-Based Rituals:**
Plants play a pivotal role in various rituals and ceremonies across different cultures and traditions. They serve as bridges connecting people to the spiritual realm, enabling us to tap into ancient wisdom and energies. Here are some examples:

- **Smudging with Sage:** The burning of sage in smudging ceremonies is a popular ritual in many Native American cultures. The smoke from the sage is believed to purify spaces, objects, and individuals from negative energies.
- **Tulsi Worship in India:** The Tulsi plant, or holy basil, is deeply revered in India. Many households have a Tulsi plant, and daily rituals involving the offering of water, lighting of lamps, and recitation of mantras are common. Special ceremonies, known as Tulsi Vivah, are even held to celebrate the divine qualities of this plant.
- **Coca Leaves in Andean Cultures:** In the Andes Mountains, indigenous people have long used coca leaves in various rituals. They believe the coca plant is a gift from the gods and use the leaves in offerings to the Earth, in divination practices, and as a sacred form of exchange between individuals.
- **Frankincense and Myrrh in Christian Traditions:** These two resins have been used in religious ceremonies for thousands of years. They were famously offered to the baby Jesus according to Christian tradition. Even today, frankincense and myrrh are used in certain Christian rituals, particularly in the Coptic and Eastern Orthodox Churches.
- **The Lotus in Buddhist Ceremonies:** The lotus flower, with its roots in the mud and blossoms rising above the water, is a powerful symbol in Buddhism. It represents purity and enlightenment. In many Buddhist ceremonies,

offerings of lotus flowers are made to statues and images of the Buddha.

- **Palo Santo in South American Rituals:** Palo Santo, or "holy wood," is a tree native to parts of South America. It is often burned similarly to sage in North American traditions. The smoke from Palo Santo is believed to have both medicinal and therapeutic healing power, as well as the ability to ward off bad spirits and energies.
- **Mistletoe in Druidic Traditions:** Ancient Druids regarded mistletoe as a sacred plant, especially when it grew on oak trees. During the winter solstice, they would hold ceremonies and harvest it, believing it had the power to bestow life and fertility, provide protection from negative forces, and heal ailments.

## Ethnobotany and Sacred Plant Traditions

Venturing deeper into the spiritual dimensions of herbalism, one can't help but marvel at the intricate tapestry of human-plant relationships that have shaped cultures, traditions, and spiritual practices across the globe. This intricate relationship is most evident in the field of ethnobotany and the sacred plant traditions that have emerged over centuries. As we journey through this article, you'll be introduced to the role of plants in indigenous spirituality, the fascinating world of shamanic practices, and the modern revival of these ancient plant rituals.

### *The Role of Plants in Indigenous Spirituality*

For millennia, the indigenous tapestry of understanding plants has been rich and profound. Beyond sustenance and medicine, plants have been silent guides, bridging the physical and spiritual realms, touching the very essence of human existence.

Indigenous societies often view the cosmos as a web of life where everything is interconnected. Plants, in this cosmology, aren't just passive entities. They're dynamic participants, playing key roles in the stories, mythologies, and rituals that define cultures.

The relationship between indigenous people and plants goes beyond mere utility. It's a bond of respect and reverence, where plants are seen as carriers of stories, history, and ancestral wisdom. They are treated as equal entities, having their own personalities, wishes, and desires.

Plants often guard the sacred knowledge of creation, healing, and transformation. They have been anointed as the keepers of secrets, revealing them only to those who approach with genuine intent. This is why many indigenous cultures have specific rituals before harvesting or using a plant, ensuring that the plant's spirit is honored and appeased.

**Examples of Indigenous Plants:**
Below are some indigenous plants that also play a role in spirituality:

- **Maize in Native American Cultures:** Maize, or corn, isn't just a staple food for many Native American tribes; it's deeply intertwined with their creation stories. The Hopi, for instance, believe that maize was given to them by Spider Woman and Tawa, the Sun Spirit, and it represents the covenant between humans and deities. Ceremonies, dances, and rituals are performed in honor of maize, celebrating its role in sustaining life.
- **The Dreamtime and Australian Bush Plants:** For Australian Aboriginal cultures, the Dreamtime represents the foundational myths and stories of their world. Plants play a significant role in these narratives. The Bush Plum, for instance, is associated with ancestral spirits and the stories of creation. It's not only a food source but also a spiritual

touchstone, reminding the people of their connection to the Dreamtime.

- **The Bamboo in Asian Traditions:** While not indigenous in the strictest sense, many Asian cultures revere bamboo as a symbol of resilience, longevity, and integrity. In traditional stories and fables, the bamboo stands firm against the strongest winds, not because it's rigid but because it bends and flexes. It's a lesson in humility, strength, and adaptability. In various ceremonies, bamboo plays a role, either as a vessel, a musical instrument, or an offering.

## *Shamanic Practices and Visionary Plants*

The canvas of shamanic traditions, painted with rituals, songs, and dances, vividly portrays the intricate relationship between humans and plants. This relationship is especially pronounced when we focus on visionary plants, nature's portals that offer glimpses into alternate dimensions of consciousness.

While many plants provide sustenance, healing, or utility, there exists a select group that shamans hold in special reverence. These plants do more than heal the body; they unlock the mind, dissolve boundaries, and propel the spirit into realms otherwise inaccessible. They are the spiritual catalysts, igniting transformative experiences.

The consumption of these plants isn't a casual affair. It's a deeply spiritual endeavor that often requires thorough preparation, including fasting, prayer, and setting clear intentions. The experiences they invoke aren't just visual; they can be emotional, psychological, and deeply introspective, prompting self-reflection and profound revelations.

## Examples of Visionary Plants

Throughout history, various cultures have utilized plants with psychoactive properties for religious, spiritual, and healing purposes. These visionary plants, often central to traditional ceremonies, are revered for their ability to induce profound psychological experiences and insights. This section explores some of the most notable visionary plants, each with a unique history and set of cultural practices surrounding their use.

- **San Pedro Cactus:** Native to the Andes mountains, the San Pedro cactus has been used for millennia in traditional Andean medicine. Its mescaline content offers transformative visions. Local shamans, or 'curanderos', use San Pedro in healing ceremonies, guiding participants through their experiences and helping them interpret their visions.
- **Magic Mushrooms (Psilocybin):** Used by various indigenous groups, particularly the Mazatec people of Mexico, these mushrooms are known to induce powerful visions. Maria Sabina, a renowned Mazatec shaman, introduced the ceremonial use of these mushrooms to the Western world. Participants often report experiences of unity, timelessness, and deep emotional release.
- **Iboga:** Beyond the previously mentioned connection to the Bwiti religion in Africa, Iboga is a powerful psychoactive root bark. Traditionally used in rites of passage and healing ceremonies, it offers visions often described as ancestral, guiding individuals through a retrospective journey, making them confront past traumas and decisions.

While the allure of these experiences is undeniable, it's essential to approach these plants with the utmost respect. They are not recreational substances but sacred tools. Always seek guidance from knowledgeable individuals and be aware of the legal and safety implications.

## Modern Revival of Ancient Plant Rituals

Amidst the whirlwind of technological advancements and the hustle of modern life, there's a palpable yearning for deeper, more meaningful connections. It is within this context that the resurgence of ancient plant rituals is gaining momentum, offering individuals a touchstone to primordial wisdom.

The modern revival of these practices isn't just a trend. It's a testament to the innate human desire for authenticity and genuine spiritual experiences. In a world often criticized for its superficiality, these plant rituals represent a counter-current, a pathway to depths of consciousness and connection that many feel are missing from modern life.

While the core of these rituals remains anchored in ancient wisdom, their modern iterations often incorporate contemporary understandings of psychology, safety, and inclusivity. This fusion ensures that the practices evolve and remain relevant, catering to the needs and sensibilities of today's seekers.

**Examples of these rituals are the following:**

- **Modern Cacao Ceremonies:** Originally practiced by ancient Mesoamerican cultures, cacao ceremonies have witnessed a global resurgence. In these ceremonies, participants drink ceremonial-grade cacao, which facilitates heart-opening experiences, introspection, and communal bonding. Today's ceremonies often blend traditional rituals with modern elements like guided meditation and group sharing.
- **Global Psilocybin Retreats:** Magic mushroom retreats have sprouted in places where the consumption of psilocybin is legal. These retreats are structured to ensure participants' safety and to provide a conducive environment for introspection. Incorporating elements like therapeutic

guidance, meditation, and integration sessions, they provide a holistic approach to the psilocybin experience.

- **Sacred Sound and Plant Integration:** Modern plant ceremonies sometimes integrate other healing modalities like sound baths, where gongs, singing bowls, and other instruments are used to enhance and guide the plant-induced journey. This multisensory approach enriches the experience, grounding participants and aiding in processing their visions.

As these practices gain popularity, it's imperative to approach them with respect and discernment. Ensuring that rituals are led by knowledgeable guides and understanding the origins and traditions behind each practice is crucial. Equally important is the need to be aware of the risks, both legal and health-related, associated with the consumption of certain plants.

## Crafting Personal Herbal Rituals

In the intricate tapestry of life, rituals are the threads that lend structure, meaning, and a sense of sacredness to our everyday existence. When woven with the magic of herbs, these rituals become profound acts of self-care, connecting us deeply to nature and our inner selves. This article delves into the art of crafting personal herbal rituals, offering a doorway to a world where the ordinary becomes extraordinary.

### *Creating Sacred Spaces with Plants*

The spaces you inhabit play a pivotal role in shaping your mental and emotional well-being. By introducing plants and herbs into these spaces, you can transform them into sanctuaries of peace, positivity, and healing. Plants are more than just decorative elements. They are living entities that resonate with energy and life force. Welcoming them into your spaces invites their vibrant energy and the age-old wisdom they carry.

**Steps to Create Your Herbal Haven:**

1. **Choosing the Right Plants:** Begin by selecting plants that resonate with your intentions. For instance, lavender promotes relaxation, while rosemary is said to enhance memory and concentration.
2. **Placement Matters:** Place the plants in areas where you spend most of your time, ensuring they receive the right amount of sunlight. Consider creating a dedicated herbal altar or a meditation corner adorned with your favorite plants.
3. **Engage All Senses:** Enhance the ambiance with aromatic herb-infused candles, herbal sachets, or essential oil diffusers. The harmonious blend of sight and scent can amplify the sacredness of your space.

## *Herbal Altars and Sacred Spaces*

The spiritual dimension of herbalism extends beyond mere consumption. It's about immersing oneself in the deeper essence of plants. Crafting a sacred space in your home, infused with the energy of specific herbs, can serve as a constant reminder of nature's gifts and mysteries. Just as altars in various traditions hold sacred items, an herbal altar showcases plants known for their spiritual and energetic properties. Here are some examples:

- **Sage, Cedar, and Sweetgrass Centerpiece:** These herbs, when combined, create a harmonious energy, inviting purification, protection, and positivity. Their dried forms, gracefully arranged, can become the heart of your altar.
- **Bowls of Calm:** Dried lavender and rose petals can be kept in decorative bowls, releasing a gentle, calming

aroma. Their mere presence can evoke feelings of tranquility and love.

## *Plant-infused Body Care Rituals*

One's body is a reflection of the soul, a physical manifestation of inner vitality. Just as plants rejuvenate the earth, plant-infused body care rituals rejuvenate the body, offering a momentary retreat from the chaos of daily life.

The simple act of touch can evoke feelings of love, warmth, and comfort. Combining this with the therapeutic properties of herbs magnifies its healing potential, turning routine body care into profound rituals of self-appreciation.

**Some Ideas for Crafting Your Ritual:**

- **Herbal Baths:** Immerse yourself in the calming waters of a warm bath infused with your choice of herbs:
  - **Chamomile:** Known for its calming properties, it helps relax the muscles and soothe the mind.
  - **Lavender:** Aids in reducing anxiety and emotional stress.
  - **Rose Petals:** Their aromatic essence uplifts the spirit and nurtures the skin.

  While in the bath, close your eyes, breathe deeply, and visualize the therapeutic energies of the herbs enveloping you, dispelling all negativity.

- **Plant-based Oils:** The post-bath ritual is just as essential. You can use these oils.
  - **Calendula Oil:** Known for its healing properties, it's excellent for sensitive or irritated skin.
  - **Arnica Oil:** Perfect for alleviating pain and inflammation.

Warm the oil between your palms and gently massage your body. Feel the herbs work their magic, rejuvenating your skin and relaxing your muscles.

- **Facial Steams:** Offer your face the gift of herbal steams. Some herbs to try are:
  - **Rosemary:** Stimulates blood circulation and aids in refreshing the skin.
  - **Eucalyptus:** Acts as a natural antiseptic, great for clearing nasal passages and reducing skin inflammation.

  Pour hot water into a bowl, add the chosen herbs, and lean over it, covering your head with a towel. Take deep breaths, allowing the steam to open up your pores and the herbal essence to cleanse them.
- **Herbal Scrubs:** Exfoliate and renew your skin with homemade herbal scrubs:
  - **Mint and Sugar Scrub:** The cooling properties of mint combined with the granular texture of sugar can leave your skin feeling refreshed.
  - **Oatmeal and Lavender Scrub:** Perfect for sensitive skin, it soothes and moisturizes.

  Gently massage the scrub onto your skin in circular motions, washing away dead skin cells and imbuing fresh energy.

## *Herbal Moments of Mindfulness*

In the fast-paced rhythm of modern life, the quest for tranquility often leads us to nature's doorstep. Mindfulness — the art of grounding oneself in the present — finds a harmonious partner in the gentle world of herbs. These plant allies don't just heal the body; they soothe the soul, beckoning us into moments of serene introspection.

When you breathe in the unique aroma of an herb, you're not just inhaling a scent; you're absorbing a story, a history, an essence.

Each breath is an intimate dance with nature, a silent dialogue that draws us into the immediate moment, shushing the clamor of external distractions.

Here are ways of incorporating herbs into mindful practices:

- **Herbal Tea Meditation:** Every cup of herbal tea is an invitation to mindfulness:
    1. Select an herb that resonates with your mood or need.
    2. Pay attention to the water's boil, the herbs' unfurl, and the color change as nature infuses its goodness into the water.
    3. As you hold the warm cup, notice its weight, the steam rising, and the aromatic whispers of the brew. Each sip is a moment of mindfulness, a chance to connect with the herb's journey from soil to cup.
- **Walking with Herbs:** Nature walks aren't just about movement; they're about immersion:
    1. As you tread gently, notice the herbs that line your path. Is it the bold rosemary or the shy violet?
    2. Take a moment to touch, to feel the life pulsing through each leaf and stem. Let these herbs anchor your senses, grounding you in the richness of the moment.
- **Journaling with Plant Essence:** Documenting one's thoughts can be a therapeutic journey in itself:
    1. As you pen down your reflections, introduce a sensory element with herb-infused inks, enhancing the tactile experience.
    2. Keep a pressed herb or flower as a bookmark. Every time you return to your journal, this botanical marker

can transport you back to the emotions and musings of that particular entry.

- **Herbal Breathing Exercises:** Turn your breathing exercises into an aromatic experience:
    1. Light an herbal incense stick, perhaps sage for clarity or sandalwood for relaxation.
    2. As you focus on your inhalation and exhalation, let the herb's aroma guide your breath, making the act even more centered and present.

# Chapter 9

# Outdoor Herbalism

This comprehensive chapter introduces you to the world of outdoor herbalism. From sustainable foraging techniques to effectively growing your herb garden, this guide aims to equip you with the knowledge to embark on the deeply fulfilling journey of connecting with herbs in their natural environment.

You will learn key identification tips to forage safely, avoiding poisonous look-alikes. The chapter also details essential tools that every forager should carry, from handy pruning shears to local plant guides. Additionally, you will discover how to make the most of your outdoor space to create a thriving herb garden.

## Foraging Herbs

Foraging for herbs is an age-old practice that has seen a resurgence in recent years. As interest in natural remedies and sustainable living grows, more and more people are turning to the wild to find medicinal plants. This section delves into the fascinating world of herb foraging, providing readers with a roadmap to embark on this rewarding journey. You will explore the importance of foraging safely and sustainably, the essential tools every forager needs, and introduce some commonly foraged medicinal herbs.

### *Safe and Sustainable Foraging Practices*

Foraging can be a deeply rewarding experience that profoundly connects you with nature. However, this connection is responsible for ensuring that your actions do not harm the environment or its inhabitants. Before venturing out to pick wild herbs, you have to understand the importance of foraging in a safe and sustainable manner. This ensures your safety and the continued abundance of medicinal plants in the environment.

- **Know Before You Go**: The first rule of foraging is always to be sure of what you pick. Some medicinal herbs have poisonous look-alikes. Before harvesting any plant, you must be 100% certain of its identity. Learning from seasoned foragers or taking a local class on plant identification is advisable.
- **Take Only What You Need**: Overharvesting can quickly deplete local populations of plants. As a rule, never take more than a third of a particular herb population. This allows the plant community to regenerate and thrive for years to come.
- **Respect Nature's Cycle**: Only harvest herbs when they are mature, and if possible, leave the roots intact. This ensures the plant can regenerate. Always remember: foraging is not just about taking but also about giving back and maintaining a balance with nature.
- **Seek Permission**: When planning to forage, ensure you have the necessary permissions. Many lands, especially protected or privately owned, may have restrictions against foraging. Always respect these boundaries to prevent legal issues and to maintain good relations with landowners or local authorities.
- **Forage Away from Polluted Areas**: It is essential to avoid collecting plants from areas that are near roadsides, industrial zones, or agricultural fields that may use pes-

ticides. Pollutants can easily get absorbed by the plants, making them unsafe for consumption. The cleaner and more untouched the environment, the healthier and more potent the herbs will be.

- **Learn the Local Ecosystem:** Different environments have varying plant species. By understanding the ecosystem of the area you are foraging, you can better anticipate what plants to expect and where to find them. For example, marshlands might be abundant in horsetail, while sunny clearings could be home to wild chamomile. Understanding this will make your foraging trip more fruitful and help you not disturb the delicate balance of the ecosystem.
- **Avoid Foraging Endangered Plants**: Some herbs are becoming rare due to various environmental and human factors. Ensure you know the local endangered plant list and avoid foraging these species. Taking such plants affects the environment and can have legal repercussions.
- **Be Cautious of Wildlife**: When out in the wild, remember you are in the habitat of various animals. Some animals, like bees or snakes, might be near the herbs you wish to forage. Always approach with caution, make your presence known *(avoid startling animals)*, and be ready to back off if you encounter a wild animal. It is their home, and they have as much right to the resources as we do.

## *Essential Gear and Tools Expanded*

Embarking on a foraging journey requires knowledge, respect for nature, and the right equipment. The tools you bring along can drastically impact the quality of your finds and the ease of your expedition. Below are essential tools and why each is crucial to the foraging process.

## Field Guides

A forager's best friend is a comprehensive field guide. These guides can be:

- **Physical books:** Handy and reliable, they often come with detailed illustrations and can be referred to even in areas without network coverage.
- **Digital apps:** Modern foraging apps can sometimes identify plants by scanning photos. They are updated regularly and can offer user reviews and real-time insights.

Whichever you choose, ensure it is specific to your region. The flora of every area is unique, and a local guide ensures accurate identification.

## Scissors or Pruners

Investing in a high-quality pair of scissors or pruners is a wise decision. Here is why:

- **Clean Cuts:** A sharp pruner ensures you cut the plant without causing unnecessary damage, essential for the plant's recovery.
- **Safety:** They help safely cut plants without hurting oneself, especially when dealing with thorny or tough plants.
- **Portability:** Modern pruners are foldable and easily fit into your pocket or bag, making them convenient to carry around.

## Collection Bags or Baskets

The receptacle you choose to store your foraged herbs in is more critical than you think.

- **Breathability:** Woven baskets or cloth bags are breathable, ensuring the collected plants remain fresh and not wilt or mold due to moisture buildup.
- **Eco-friendliness:** Cloth bags and baskets are sustainable options compared to plastic bags, aligning with the foraging ethos.
- **Sorting Ease:** Baskets, in particular, allow you to lay your finds flat, minimizing damage and making it easier to sort through them later.

## Notebooks and Pens

A foraging trip is as much about the experience as the finds. Maintaining a diary can have several advantages:

- **Memory Aid:** Recording each plant's specifics helps reinforce memory and aids in quicker identification in future trips.
- **Location Tracker:** By noting where you found a particular herb, you can easily revisit the spot.
- **Personal Growth:** Over time, reviewing your notes can show how much you have learned and grown as a forager. It is also a beautiful way to relive past expeditions.
- **Sharing Knowledge:** Your experiences and notes can be invaluable to other budding foragers. Sharing your diary or notes can help build a community of responsible and knowledgeable foragers.

## *Commonly Foraged Medicinal Herbs*

Nature's pharmacy is vast; its aisles are the forests, meadows, and backyards. The plants that many overlook can be medicinal treasures waiting to be discovered. In this section, delve into some commonly foraged medicinal herbs, their identification features, and their health benefits.

### Dandelion (Taraxacum Officinale)

Dandelions are easily recognizable with their bright yellow flowers and serrated green leaves. Once the flower has bloomed, it turns into a white, fluffy seed head, often blown away by the wind or children making a wish.

Dandelion leaves are not just edible but are nutrition-packed and rich in vitamins A, C, and K. When dried and roasted, the roots can be used as a coffee substitute. Dandelions are believed to act as diuretics, support liver function, and aid digestion. They are also known to contain antioxidants that can help reduce inflammation.

### Plantain (Plantago Major)

Plantain has broad, oval leaves with veins parallel to the leaf margins. When it flowers, you will notice a tall spike covered in tiny, densely packed flowers shooting up from the center.

Plantain leaves have been traditionally used for wound healing due to their antimicrobial properties. They can be crushed into a paste and applied to wounds, insect bites, or stings to alleviate pain and inflammation. Plantain tea can also soothe sore throats and coughs.

### St. John's Wort (Hypericum Perforatum)

This plant bears bright yellow flowers with numerous stamens in the center. When the petals are crushed, they leave a red residue, a distinguishing feature.

St. John's Wort has historically been used for its potential mood-lifting properties. Extracts from this herb have been employed in traditional medicine to manage symptoms of mild to moderate depression. However, it is crucial to consult with a medical professional before using it, especially if you are on other medications.

### Nettle (Urtica Dioica)

Nettle plants have jagged-edged leaves and tiny, hair-like structures that deliver a stinging sensation when touched.

Once cooked or dried, the nettle loses its sting and reveals its nutritional bounty. Rich in iron, magnesium, calcium, and other nutrients, nettle tea can help combat fatigue, reduce inflammation, and support joint health. Nettle soup is also a traditional favorite in many cultures.

## Identifying Wild Toxic Herbs

While the wild offers an array of beneficial herbs with healing properties, it also harbors dangerously toxic plants. Recognizing and avoiding these harmful plants is crucial for anyone venturing into herbalism.

### *The Importance of Proper Identification*

Stepping into the world of wild plants is akin to entering a vast library, where each plant tells a story. But without the right skills to 'read' them, you might find yourself 'reading' a dangerous tale. Let us navigate the intricacies of identifying toxic herbs and ensure your foraging journey is safe and enlightening.

#### Look-alikes are Deceptive

Imagine picking up a delicious-looking fruit only to realize it is an imposter! In the plant kingdom, appearances can be highly deceptive.

Start by studying one plant family at a time. Familiarize yourself with its common members, both safe and toxic. Over time, you will start noticing subtle differences between good and bad.

Nature has a quirky sense of humor; many beneficial plants have toxic doppelgangers. It is like trying to find a genuine painting in a room filled with expert forgeries. It is a game of details. The minute characteristics, from stem textures to leaf arrangements, can be the difference between a delightful herbal remedy and a medical emergency. Always double-check, and when in doubt, just throw it out.

Here are some examples of herbs and their deceptive look-alikes.

#### *Wild Carrot vs. Poison Hemlock*

Wild Carrot, also known as Queen Anne's Lace, is often sought after for its delicate flowers and carrot-scented root. However, it has a dangerous look-alike: the Poison Hemlock. While Wild Carrot has hairy stems, Poison Hemlock stems are smooth with purplish blotches. Consuming even a small amount of the latter can be deadly.

**Tip:** *Rub the leaves and take a whiff. Wild Carrot has a distinct carrot smell, while Poison Hemlock has a musty odor.*

### *Mint vs. Pennyroyal*

Both members of the mint family, these plants can be mistaken due to their similar appearance. While many mint varieties are beloved for their refreshing taste and aroma, Pennyroyal has a high concentration of pulegone, which can be toxic when consumed in large quantities.

**Tip:** *Feel the stem. Mint stems are square-shaped, while those of Pennyroyal are round.*

### *Elderberry vs. Water Hemlock*

Elderberries are popularly harvested for syrups, wines, and jams. However, they can be mistaken for the highly toxic Water Hemlock. While Elderberries have a woody stem, Water Hemlock has green stems with purple striations.

**Tip:** *Check the berry clusters. Elderberries droop or hang downwards, whereas Water Hemlock's smaller berry clusters stand upright.*

## Know Your Regional Variations

You might have a friend from another state rave about a beneficial herb, but that does not mean it is safe in your region. Plants vary regionally, and so do their toxic counterparts. Invest in a localized plant guidebook. These regional guidebooks often provide detailed images and descriptions, helping you discern between safe and harmful plants in your area.

## Be Careful of Poisonous Plants

Some plants have evolved to contain toxins to ward off predators. When encountering an unknown plant, avoid the urge to taste test. While it might seem fun, it is not worth the potential risk. Always be cautious, even if the plant looks inviting.

## Consult Experts

There is a vast community of herbalists, botanists, and foragers who have trodden the path you are on. Their expertise can be invaluable, especially when you are unsure. Join local foraging or plant identification workshops. These often involve guided walks where experts point out local flora, discussing their benefits and dangers. Not only do you learn, but you also get hands-on experience, making it easier to remember. Alternatively, consider joining online forums or social media groups dedicated to foraging in your region. Sharing pictures and asking questions there can be incredibly enlightening.

### *Characteristics of Common Toxic Plants*

Venturing into the wild to collect herbs might feel like an adventurous treasure hunt, but it is essential to recognize the difference between genuine treasure and fool's gold. To help you navigate this vast green library, we have categorized toxic plants based on their tell-tale characteristics.

## Unpleasant or Peculiar Smell

Mother Nature has her way of warning potential foragers. A plant's scent can be a big giveaway.

- **Hemlock (Conium maculatum):** Resembling wild carrots, Hemlock is distinguishable by its foul smell when crushed. It has smooth stems with purple-red spots, whereas wild carrots have hairy stems. A small bite can have dire consequences.

- **Ragwort (Senecio jacobaea):** Often found in fields, its leaves give off an unpleasant smell when crushed. Though its bright yellow flowers might seem inviting, consuming this plant can lead to liver damage.

***Tip:*** *Always give unfamiliar plants a gentle crush and sniff test. A sharp, unpleasant odor is often nature's "do not eat" sign.*

## Shiny and Tempting Berries

Remember the saying, *"All that glitters is not gold"?* It applies to berries, too. As a general rule, always be wary of brightly colored, shiny berries. They are nature's jewels but not always meant for consumption.

- **Belladonna (Atropa belladonna):** Its shiny, dark purple berries might look delicious but extremely toxic. Even a few can cause dizziness, increased heartbeat, and blurred vision.
- **Pokeweed (Phytolacca americana):** This plant produces shiny, deep purple-black berries, tempting but toxic. Consuming them can cause severe digestive distress.

## Alluring and Beautiful Flowers

Beauty can be deceptive, and some of the most gorgeous flowers can be the most dangerous in the plant world.

- **Foxglove (Digitalis purpurea):** Its captivating tall spikes of purple-pink flowers might draw you in, but all its parts are highly toxic. Consuming it can affect the heart.

- **Oleander (Nerium oleander):** Widely used as an ornamental plant, its beautiful flowers come in various colors. However, every bit of it, from stem to petals, is poisonous.

### Milky or Discolored Sap

Some toxic plants exude a milky sap when broken, often a sign of caution.

- **Giant Hogweed (Heracleum mantegazzianum):** Breaking its stem or leaves releases a sap that can cause severe skin burns when exposed to sunlight.
- **Euphorbia (Euphorbia spp.):** Many plants in this genus release a milky, latex-like sap when broken. Some species' sap can irritate the skin and become toxic if ingested.

***Tip:*** *If a plant oozes a milky or strangely colored sap, it is best to avoid it, especially if you are unfamiliar with its properties. Always wear gloves when handling unknown plants.*

## *Responding to Accidental Ingestion*

Imagine you are out in the wild, enjoying the tranquility of nature, when someone accidentally munches on an unknown plant. The initial reaction might be to panic, but knowing the proper steps can be life-saving. This guide aims to provide a structured approach in such scenarios.

### Stay Calm

The first response in any emergency is often panic, but maintaining composure has a ripple effect. It not only allows you to think clearly but also helps in keeping the affected person calm. Practice deep breathing exercises to steady your nerves. This might sound mundane, but returning to your breath can anchor you in high-stress situations.

## Eliminate the Culprit

If the person is conscious and coherent, gently encourage them to spit out any remaining parts of the plant from their mouth. If possible, rinse the mouth with water to remove any lingering toxins. Always carry a small bottle of water with you during foraging trips. Apart from hydration, it can come in handy in such situations.

## Gather Information

Dial emergency services or your local poison control center without delay. While waiting, try to collect a sample or take a clear photo of the ingested plant. This can help medical personnel identify and determine the best course of action. To collect samples, equip yourself with a small, sealable plastic bag during foraging trips. It is lightweight and can be crucial in emergencies.

## Induce Vomit

There is a common misconception that vomiting should be the immediate response after ingesting something toxic. However, some plants can cause more damage when they come back up, burning the esophagus or releasing more toxins. It is essential to have guidance on this step. Only induce vomiting if instructed by a medical professional.

## Continuous Monitoring

Until medical help arrives, closely monitor the affected person. Note any changes in their behavior, physical symptoms, or level of consciousness. This information can be valuable to medical teams. If you are in a group, delegate tasks. While one person contacts emergency services, another can attend to the affected individual, ensuring they are comfortable and not alone.

## Cultivating an Outdoor Herb Garden

Herbs, with their enticing aromas and myriad uses, have enthralled humankind for eons. Cultivating your outdoor herb garden gives you a direct supply of these beneficial plants and immerses you in a world of freshness, fragrance, and healing. Whether you are a city dweller with just a balcony or sprawling acres, starting an herb garden can be fulfilling. This section sets the foundation for your green endeavors.

### *Understanding Your Space*

Every patch of land, no matter how small, has its own unique set of characteristics. Understanding these factors, from varying degrees of sunlight to diverse soil compositions, is the key to unlocking your garden's potential.

#### Sunlight Matters

Every herb has its preference when it comes to sunlight. However, a majority bask in the sun's glory. Take note of these considerations:

- **Daily Dose of Vitamin D**: Ensure your chosen spot is not shaded for long periods. Most herbs thrive with a minimum of 6 hours of direct sunlight.
- **Partial Shade Considerations**: Some herbs, like parsley or mint, can tolerate partial shade. So, if you are dealing with limited sun, these can be your go-to herbs.

Use a sun calculator or simply observe your garden space at different times of the day to determine the sunniest spots.

## Know Your Soil

Soil is the lifeblood of your garden, nourishing your plants with essential nutrients. Listed below are some tips:

- **Texture and Composition**: Soil can be sandy, loamy, or clayey. While sandy soil ensures good drainage, clayey soil retains moisture. Ideally, herbs prefer a loamy mix, which is a balanced combination.
- **pH Level**: Herbs generally prefer a neutral pH. Consider getting a soil testing kit to determine your soil's pH level, adjusting it, if necessary, with lime *(to raise pH)* or sulfur *(to lower pH)*.
- **Amending Your Soil**: If soil retains too much water, it can be a breeding ground for diseases. Improve its drainage by adding organic matter like compost or sand.
- **Use Compost:** Regularly enrich your soil with homemade compost. It not only boosts soil health but also recycles kitchen waste.

## Adapting to Challenges:

Not everyone has the luxury of a vast garden. But limited space should not limit your aspirations. Some ideas include:

- **Container Gardening**: If ground space is scarce, consider container gardening. Many herbs adapt beautifully to pots and can be arranged aesthetically on patios, balconies, or window sills.
- **Vertical Gardening**: Make use of vertical spaces. Wall-mounted planters or stacked pots can be an innovative way to grow herbs.

**Tip**: *Choose containers with adequate drainage holes. Overwatering is a common mistake in container gardening, and proper drainage can mitigate this risk.*

## *Planting and Care*

Entering the world of gardening means becoming a plant parent. Every sprout and seedling under your care will rely on you for its growth and well-being. But fret not, for with some knowledge and dedication, you can help your green babies thrive using the tips below.

### Spacing

Just like we need our personal space to flourish, plants, too, seek their little corner in the sun. Planting herbs too close can make their roots compete for space and nutrients. For instance, robust growers like mint can overshadow others without their own space. Before planting, research each herb's growth pattern. This can help you plot out an optimal layout for your garden, ensuring each plant gets its bubble.

### Watering

Water is life, but too much or too little can spell disaster for your plants. Rather than frequent shallow watering, opt for deep watering sessions. This ensures the water reaches the deeper roots, promoting robust root systems. Overwatered plants may have yellow leaves, while underwatered ones may have dry, brown edges. Adjust your watering routine accordingly. Consider investing in a water meter. It takes the guesswork out of watering, allowing you to gauge the moisture levels in the soil accurately.

### Fending Off Pests

No matter how well-tended, every garden will face its fair share of pesky invaders. You can naturally solve this problem by using these:

- **Natural Deterrents**: Plants like marigolds and lavender naturally repel certain pests. Intersperse them among your herbs as a fragrant defense line.
- **Beneficial Insects**: Not all bugs are bad. Ladybugs, for instance, are natural predators of many garden pests. By creating a welcoming environment, you can enlist their help keeping pests at bay.

***Tip:*** *Regularly inspect the underside of leaves. Many pests, like aphids, often hide there. Early detection can prevent larger infestations.*

### Feeding Your Plants

Like all plants, herbs need nutrients to grow and produce aromatic leaves you cherish. Here are some tips:

- **Composting**: Regularly amending your soil with compost enhances its texture and infuses it with vital nutrients.
- **Organic Fertilizers**: These are gentle on the plants and introduce nutrients slowly, reducing the risk of over-fertilization. Avoid synthetic fertilizers that can harm the natural soil ecosystem. Instead, opt for seaweed solutions or worm castings as natural nutrient boosters.

## *Harvesting and Storage*

Harvesting is a joyous occasion for every gardener, the culmination of weeks or even months of hard work. However, to ensure that you get the best out of your plants, you must approach this stage with care and knowledge.

## Timing Matters

Just as planting and watering have their ideal moments, so does harvesting. For most herbs, just before they flower, they are at their most potent in terms of flavor and medicinal properties. For instance, harvesting just before the buds fully open will give you the most aromatic brew if you are growing chamomile for tea. Take note of the time of the day when harvesting. As the saying goes, the early bird gets the worm, or in this case, the most flavorful herbs. Harvesting post-dew and pre-heat of the day ensures you capture the plant's essence at its peak.

## The Right Harvesting Technique

Your plants have been your babies; treat them with care even during harvesting.

First, you should prune and do not pluck: Pulling can damage the roots. Always use a sharp tool to make clean cuts. Avoid overharvesting: Never take more than a third of the plant. This ensures it can recover and continue to grow.

For instance, with basil, regular pruning encourages bushier growth, yielding more leaves in the long run. Lastly, regularly sharpen your shears or scissors to ensure clean cuts every time. This helps in preventing infections and promotes faster healing of the plant.

## Storage Solutions

If you have harvested a bounty, use them immediately in your dishes to elevate the taste. Nothing beats the flavor of freshly plucked herbs. But if not using immediately, how do you keep it fresh? Here are some tips:

- **Drying and Dehydrating**: Some herbs, like oregano or thyme, can be dried and stored for long-term use. Tie them in bundles and hang them upside down in a dry, airy space. Alternatively, using a dehydrator can speed up the process.
- **Freezing for Freshness**: Herbs like basil and parsley can be chopped, placed in ice cube trays with water, and frozen. Pop an herb cube in your cooking for freshness any time of the year.
- **Store in Cool Location:** For those herbs that prefer cooler storage, wrapping them in a slightly damp paper towel and placing them in a sealable bag in the refrigerator can extend their freshness. Periodically check for any signs of mold or wilting and use them before they go bad.

## Exercise: Herbal Scavenger Hunt and Identification Journal

This activity aims to enhance your ability to identify, understand, and record medicinal and toxic herbs in a safe and sustainable manner while also familiarizing yourself with the natural environments where they grow.

**Materials:**

- A notebook or journal
- A camera or smartphone
- Field guide on local plants or herbs *(or a reliable plant identification app)*
- Essential foraging gear as mentioned in the chapter *(gloves, small shears, containers, etc.)*

**Instructions:**

1. **Preparation:** Familiarize yourself with the basics of safe and sustainable foraging. This includes understanding the essential gear needed, respecting nature, and the importance of accurate plant identification for safety.
2. **Location:** Find a local natural area suitable for foraging, such as a forest, meadow, or another natural habitat. Ensure you are aware of and follow local regulations about foraging in that area.
3. **Scavenger List Creation:** Based on information from your field guide or app, compile a list of 3 to 5 medicinal herbs and 2 to 3 toxic herbs that are likely to be found in your chosen location.
4. **Field Trip:** Equip yourself with your list, journal, camera, and foraging gear. Go to your selected location. Always prioritize safety during your exploration.
5. **Herbal Hunt:** As you traverse the area:
    a. Search for the herbs on your list.
    b. When you spot one, photograph it.
    c. Note the date, location, and the plant's distinguishing characteristics in your journal.
    d. If permitted and safe, collect a small sample, ensuring you adhere to respectful and sustainable foraging guidelines.
6. **Research and Reflect:** Upon returning:
    a. Match your samples and photos with your field guide or app to verify your identification.
    b. In your journal, write about any uncertainties, challenges, or unique observations you encountered.
    c. If you have kept samples, consider pressing them into your journal for future reference.

7. **Bonus Action:** Try using one of the medicinal herbs in a basic homemade preparation, such as tea. Document the process and any observations in your journal.

**Note:** Never consume or use any wild plant unless you know its identity and safe usage. When unsure, seek guidance from a knowledgeable herbalist or botanist.

# Conclusion

In the rapidly evolving world, where technology often overshadows nature's whispers, you have embarked on a profound journey back to the earth and its abundant remedies. This book was designed to serve as a beacon, illuminating the timeless wisdom and virtues of herbal remedies and natural medicines.

From the ancient practices cherished by our ancestors to the sustainable solutions for our modern ailments, we have spanned continents and eras, examining the rich tapestry of herbalism. Your exploration covered holistic healing techniques, insights for family health, practices for daily well-being, and even solutions for our beloved pets. Through each chapter, I sought to guide you closer to the heart of nature, helping bridge the gap between ancient wisdom and contemporary needs.

As the final pages of this guide draw to a close, my commitment to you stands fulfilled. I aimed to provide both understanding and actionable knowledge, and I hope this book has been your compass, leading you toward a holistic and harmonious lifestyle.

Above all, the enduring message I hope remains etched in your heart is the power of nature's simplicity. In the delicate balance of herbs and their myriad properties lies the potential to transform, heal, and rejuvenate. As you step forward on your health journey, let the boundless wisdom of nature be your guide, and remember: *true healing and vitality often emerge from the very essence of the earth we cherish.*

# Technique Recap

The following are the techniques and tips found in ***"Herbal Remedies & Natural Medicine Essentials [All in 1]"*:**

| # | Technique / Hack | Explanation |
|---|---|---|
| 1 | Heat Protection for Jars | Ensure the jars are kept in cupboards or drawers away from heat sources, like stoves or ovens, as heat can degrade herbs. |
| 2 | Selecting the Right Jars | When opting for glass jars, ensure they have a tight-sealing lid. Mason jars or similar jars with rubber gaskets and clasp closures are especially good. |
| 3 | Labeling Best Practices | Use clear, legible writing, and if possible, use waterproof labels or markers. Including both the common name and the Latin name of the herb can be helpful, especially for multiple varieties. |
| 4 | Freezing Herbs | When freezing herbs, you can either store them whole or chop them up and store them in ice cube trays with a bit of water or oil. |
| 5 | Dosage for Beginners | For those new to herbal remedies, it's always wise to start with a lower dosage and observe how your body reacts. |
| 6 | Dosage Adjustments | Children or individuals with lower body weights generally require smaller doses. |
| 7 | Understanding Herb Potency | The potency of an herb can vary depending on its form. Dried herbs might require a different dosage than tinctures or extracts. Always refer to guidelines specific to the form you're using. |

| # | Technique / Hack | Explanation |
|---|---|---|
| 8 | Consistency in Herbal Remedies | Herbal remedies often work best when taken consistently over time rather than in large, sporadic doses. |
| 9 | Investing in a Field Guide | Invest in a good field guide specific to your region for clear photographs and descriptions, aiding accurate identification. |
| 10 | Learning from Local Experts | Local herbalists or botanists often conduct workshops for learning to recognize both beneficial and toxic plants in your area. |
| 11 | Medication and Supplement List | Always keep an updated list of all the medications and supplements you're taking. This will be handy if you consult a professional. |
| 12 | Stay Informed on Interactions | New research is continually shedding light on potential interactions. Regularly updating your knowledge can help in safe usage. |
| 13 | Monitoring for Allergic Reactions | Pay attention to any unusual symptoms after consuming an herb, such as itching, hives, swelling, or respiratory issues. These might be signs of an allergic reaction. |
| 14 | Performing a Patch Test | For topical herbal products, perform a patch test by applying a small amount to a patch of skin and waiting 24 hours to check for any reactions. |
| 15 | Knowing Allergy-Prone Herbs | Some herbs are more likely to cause allergic reactions than others. Know the common culprits. |
| 16 | Clear Usage Methods | Some herbs are more suitable for topical application, while others can be consumed. You should be clear about the method of use. |
| 17 | Monitoring Children for Allergies | If using herbal remedies on children, always monitor them for any allergic reactions when introducing a new herbal remedy. Signs might include skin rashes or difficulty breathing. |

| # | Technique / Hack | Explanation |
|---|---|---|
| 18 | Proper Storage | Store all herbal products in a cool, dry place, away from direct sunlight and out of the reach of children to prevent accidental misuse. |
| 19 | Fresh Herbs in Cooking | Chop fresh herbs and sprinkle them over salads, pizzas, or sandwiches for enhanced flavor. |
| 20 | Incorporating Herbs in Cooking | Incorporate herbs like rosemary, thyme, or oregano into stews, soups, or sauces to impart deeper flavor profiles. |
| 21 | Using Herb-Infused Oils | Drizzling herb-infused oils over dishes can provide an instant flavor boost. |
| 22 | Herbs in Marinades and Dressings | Infuse herbs into marinades and dressings to elevate the flavor of meats and salads. |
| 23 | Cleaning Herbs | Always wash and pat dry your herbs before using them in cooking to ensure they're free from any dirt or pesticides. |
| 24 | Herbs in Smoothies and Juices | Blend herbs into smoothies and juices, such as parsley for detoxification or basil for its anti-inflammatory properties. |
| 25 | Morning Ritual with Green Tea | Start your day with a warm cup of green tea to ingest antioxidants and embrace a moment of mindfulness. |
| 26 | Diluting Essential Oils | Always dilute essential oils using a carrier oil for topical applications and ensure proper dispersion when diffusing. |
| 27 | Creating Herbal Sachets | Make sachets filled with dried aromatic herbs to place in drawers, closets, or cars for a subtle scent. |
| 28 | Choosing Hydrosols for Sensitive Noses | For those sensitive to strong scents, opt for hydrosols, which are gentler aromatic waters derived from distilling plant materials. |
| 29 | Watering Techniques | Before watering, check the soil's moisture by sticking your finger in up to an inch deep. Water only if it feels dry. |

| # | Technique / Hack | Explanation |
|---|---|---|
| 30 | Watering at the Base | It's best to water the base of the plant to prevent fungal issues on the leaves and ensure excess water can escape in pots without saucers to avoid root rot. |
| 31 | Humidity for Herbs | Some herbs, like basil, thrive in higher humidity. Use a tray filled with water and pebbles near your plants to increase ambient moisture in drier conditions. |
| 32 | Optimal Harvest Time | The best time for harvesting is early morning when the plant's essential oils are most concentrated. |
| 33 | Using Clean Cutting Tools | Use a sharp, clean pair of scissors or pruners for harvesting to reduce stress on the plant and prevent damage. |
| 34 | Sustainable Harvesting | Allow your plant enough leaves for photosynthesis during harvest to ensure sustained growth and repeated harvests. |
| 35 | Hydration During Detox | Drink plenty of water, especially during fasting and detoxification, to assist in toxin elimination and prevent dehydration. |
| 36 | Ethical Wild Harvesting | Never take more than a third of a particular herb population when wild harvesting to allow the plant community to regenerate and thrive. |
| 37 | Safe Harvesting Locations | Avoid collecting plants from areas near roadsides, industrial zones, or agricultural fields that may use pesticides. |
| 38 | Wildlife Safety | When foraging, make your presence known to avoid startling wildlife, and be prepared to back off if you encounter a wild animal. |
| 39 | Beware of Brightly Colored Berries | As a general rule, be wary of brightly colored, shiny berries which may indicate toxicity. |
| 40 | Utilizing Deep Breathing | Practice deep breathing exercises to steady your nerves, especially useful in high-stress situations as a grounding technique. |

| # | Technique / Hack | Explanation |
|---|---|---|
| 41 | Immediate Response to Toxic Ingestion | If someone ingests a toxic herb, encourage them to spit out any remaining plant parts and rinse their mouth if coherent and conscious. |
| 42 | Emergency Response | In case of toxic ingestion, dial emergency services or your local poison control center immediately, and try to provide a sample or photo of the ingested plant. |
| 43 | Selecting a Sunny Spot for Herb Gardens | When cultivating an outdoor herb garden, choose a spot that receives a minimum of 6 hours of direct sunlight. |
| 44 | Herbs for Partial Shade | If dealing with limited sunlight, opt for herbs like parsley or mint that can tolerate partial shade. |
| 45 | Container Gardening | Consider container gardening for herbs if ground space is scarce. Many herbs adapt well to pots and can be arranged aesthetically. |
| 46 | Utilizing Vertical Spaces | Make use of vertical spaces with wall-mounted planters or stacked pots for an innovative way to grow herbs. |
| 47 | Pest Inspection | Regularly inspect the underside of leaves for pests like aphids. Early detection can prevent larger infestations. |
| 48 | Natural Fertilizers | Opt for natural nutrient boosters like seaweed solutions or worm castings, avoiding synthetic fertilizers that harm the soil ecosystem. |

# References

Ayisi, E. O. (1992). *An Introduction to the Study of African Culture.* East African Publishers.

Bivins, R. (2010). *Alternative Medicine?* A History. OUP Oxford.

Bone, K. (2003). *A Clinical Guide to Blending Liquid Herbs: Herbal Formulations for the Individual Patient.* Elsevier Health Sciences.

Chevallier, A. (2016). *Encyclopedia of Herbal Medicine: 550 Herbs and Remedies for Common Ailments.* National Geographic Books.

Davidson, J. (2013). *Health Benefits of Rosemary For Cooking and Health.* JD-Biz Corp Publishing.

Gamlin, L. (2000). *Food Allergies and Food Intolerance: The Complete Guide to Their Identification and Treatment.* In J. Brostoff (Ed.), Inner Traditions / Bear & Co.

Garran, T. A. (2008). *Western Herbs according to Traditional Chinese Medicine: A Practitioner's Guide.* Simon and Schuster.

Hallowell, M. (1994). *Herbal Healing: A Practical Introduction to Medicinal Herbs.* Avery Publishing Group.

Hubert, A. (2020). *Herbal Medicine for Beginners: The Secret of Herbal Medicine and the Power to Heal You - What Everybody Ought to Know About Herbalism, Herbal Remedies, And How to Be Your Own Herbalist.* Independently Published.

Kandel, I. (2005). *Principles of Holistic Medicine: Quality of Life and Health.* In S. Ventegodt (Ed.), Trafford Publishing.

Kucera, S. (2022). *The Seven Ways of Ayurveda: Discover Your Dosha, Tap Into Your Strengths—and Thrive in Work, Love, and Life.* The Experiment.

Maciocia, G. (2015). *The Foundations of Chinese Medicine: A Comprehensive Text.* Elsevier Health Sciences.

Marsden, K. (2010). *Good Gut Healing: The no-nonsense guide to bowel & digestive disorders.* Little, Brown Book Group.

McGuffin, M. (1997). *Botanical Safety Handbook.* CRC Press.

Muskin, P. R. (2008). *Complementary and Alternative Medicine and Psychiatry.* American Psychiatric Pub.

Phillips Rnd, E. (2020). *Food Preservation Techniques: The Beginners Approach to Food Preservation, The Step-by-Step Instructions on How to Freeze, Dry, Can, and Preserve Food.* Amazon Digital Services LLC - KDP Print US.

Popham, S. (2019). *Evolutionary Herbalism: Science, Spirituality, and Medicine from the Heart of Nature.* North Atlantic Books.

Prabhakar, P. K. (2022). *Herb-Drug Combinations: A New Complementary Therapeutic Strategy.* In S. Hemaiswarya (Ed.), Springer Nature.

Rose, K. M. (2022). *The Art & Practice of Spiritual Herbalism: Transform, Heal, and Remember with the Power of Plants and Ancestral Medicine.* Fair Winds Press.

Schulz, K. (2023). *Spiritual Herbalism: The Power of Plants & Ancestral Medicine.* Kourtney Schulz.

Selin, H. (2006). *Medicine Across Cultures: History and Practice of Medicine in Non-Western Cultures.* Springer Science & Business Media.

Tierra, M. (2018). *Planetary Herbology.* Lotus Press.

Van Arsdall, A. (2012). *Medieval Herbal Remedies: The Old English Herbarium and Anglo-Saxon Medicine.* Routledge.

Wachtel-Galor, S. (2011). *Herbal Medicine: Biomolecular and Clinical Aspects,* Second Edition. In I. F. F. Benzie (Ed.), CRC Press.

Walker, C. (2003). *Understanding Skin Problems: Acne, Eczema, Psoriasis and Related Conditions.* In L. Papadopoulos (Ed.), John Wiley & Sons.

# Exclusive Bonuses

Dear Reader,

As we wrap up our journey through the enriching world of herbalism, I am thrilled to present you with a collection of carefully curated bonuses. These resources are designed to deepen your connection with nature and enhance your understanding of herbalism's vast potential for wellness, creativity, and spiritual growth.

- **Bonus 1 - Nature's Elixir: Herbal Cosmetics and Beauty Recipes for Radiant Wellness**
  Dive into the world of natural beauty with this comprehensive guide to herbal cosmetics. Discover recipes and techniques for creating your own herbal skincare and beauty products, each designed to harness the healing and rejuvenating properties of plants for radiant wellness.

- **Bonus 2 - Herbalism and Mental Health: Nurturing the Mind with Nature's Gifts**
  Explore the profound connection between herbalism and mental well-being in this insightful resource. Learn how herbs can support emotional balance, stress relief, and mental clarity, offering a gentle, holistic approach to nurturing your mind.

- **Bonus 3 - Herbal Wisdom for Emotional Healing: Tools and Practices for Inner Harmony**
  Gain deeper insights into the emotional healing aspects of herbalism with this bonus. It provides practical tools and meditative practices that integrate herbal wisdom, enhancing your journey toward inner harmony and resilience.

- **Bonus 4 - Botanical Creations: Herbal Art and Craft Projects for Nature Lovers**
  Unleash your creativity with this guide to herbal art and craft projects. From herbal dyes to botanical papermaking, these projects merge the beauty of herbs with artistic expression, perfect for nature enthusiasts and crafters alike.

- **Bonus 5 - Cosmic Botanica: Exploring the Celestial Power of Herbal Astrology**
  Venture into the mystical realm where herbalism meets astrology. This unique guide offers insights into how the movements of the planets and stars influence the herbal world, providing a celestial perspective on plant-based healing.

**How to Access Your Bonuses:**
Scan the QR Code Below: Use your smartphone's camera or a QR code scanner app to access these bonuses instantly.

Visit the Link: Alternatively, you can explore these valuable resources by visiting this link. bit.ly/Brown-HRNM

These bonuses are my gift to you, in gratitude for joining me on this herbal voyage. May they inspire you to further integrate the wisdom of plants into your life, crafting a path of wellness that is in harmony with the natural world.

With warmest regards,

*Astrid Brown*

Made in the USA
Monee, IL
18 December 2025

39093847R00098